Early Christianity

An Enthralling Overview of Jesus, the Twelve Apostles, the Conversion of Constantine, and Other Events in Christian History

© Copyright 2024 - All rights reserved.

The content contained within this book may not be reproduced, duplicated, or transmitted without direct written permission from the author or the publisher.

Under no circumstances will any blame or legal responsibility be held against the publisher, or author, for any damages, reparation, or monetary loss due to the information contained within this book, either directly or indirectly.

Legal Notice:

This book is copyright protected. It is only for personal use. You cannot amend, distribute, sell, use, quote, or paraphrase any part, or the content within this book, without the consent of the author or publisher.

Disclaimer Notice:

Please note the information contained within this document is for educational and entertainment purposes only. All effort has been executed to present accurate, up-to-date, reliable, and complete information. No warranties of any kind are declared or implied. Readers acknowledge that the author is not engaging in the rendering of legal, financial, medical, or professional advice. The content within this book has been derived from various sources. Please consult a licensed professional before attempting any techniques outlined in this book.

By reading this document, the reader agrees that under no circumstances is the author responsible for any losses, direct or indirect, that are incurred as a result of the use of the information contained within this document, including, but not limited to, errors, omissions, or inaccuracies.

Free limited time bonus

Stop for a moment. We have a free bonus set up for you. The problem is this: we forget 90% of everything that we read after 7 days. Crazy fact, right? Here's the solution: we've created a printable, 1-page pdf summary for this book that you're reading now. All you have to do to get your free pdf summary is to go to the following website:

https://livetolearn.lpages.co/enthrallinghistory/

Once you do, it will be intuitive. Enjoy, and thank you!

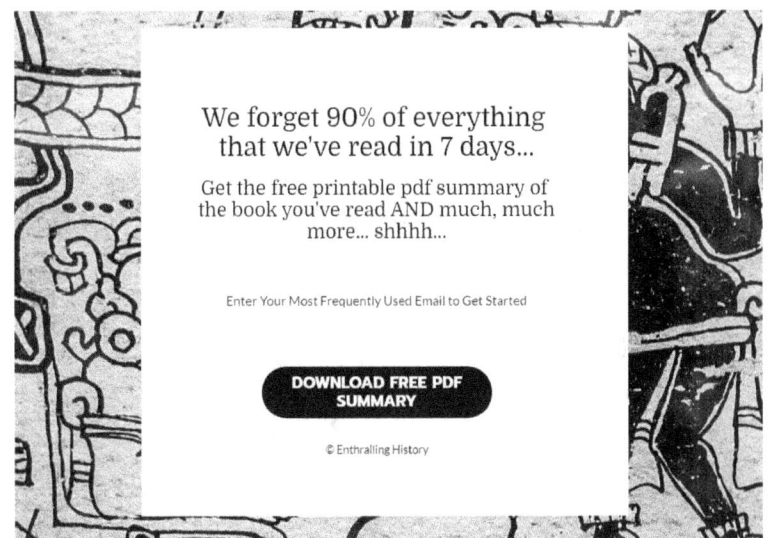

Table of Contents

INTRODUCTION 1
CHAPTER 1: ORIGINS AND BACKGROUND 3
CHAPTER 2: THE GOSPELS 11
CHAPTER 3: THE APOSTLES' MISSIONS 30
CHAPTER 4: THE FIRST CHURCH 39
CHAPTER 5: EARLY CHRISTIAN COMMUNITIES 43
CHAPTER 6: REMOVAL OF JEWISH CHARACTERISTICS 49
CHAPTER 7: ONE RELIGION, MANY VERSIONS 53
CHAPTER 8: THE FIRST CHURCH FATHERS 59
CHAPTER 9: WOMEN OF CHRISTIANITY 72
CHAPTER 10: PERSECUTIONS 83
CHAPTER 11: CONSTANTINE'S CONTRIBUTION 92
CHAPTER 12: STATE RELIGION AND HERESIES 100
CHAPTER 13: MONASTICISM AND ASCETICISM 103
CHAPTER 14: WESTERN MISSIONARY EXPANSION AND THE PAPACY 110
BONUS CHAPTER: ART 117
CONCLUSION 124
HERE'S ANOTHER BOOK BY ENTHRALLING HISTORY THAT YOU MIGHT LIKE 126
FREE LIMITED TIME BONUS 127
REFERENCES 128

Introduction

A savior, a prophet, a good man—despite varying opinions about what role Jesus filled, history agrees on his existence and the impact his words had on the world. What he taught revolutionized the Jewish world of his time. Why? What was so profound about his existence and teachings that thousands of people changed their lives and the way they worshiped?

It is important to understand the Jewish position, thinking, and culture of the time. They were waiting for someone who would save them, but from what? And did Jesus fulfill their expectations? The historical context surrounding the years before and not long after Jesus was born help us gain insight into why Jesus was such an important figure and how the political and social climate affected the birth of Christianity.

This journey through early Christianity will start about one hundred years before Jesus was born and discuss some of the most notable aspects of his life and his teachings. It will continue through what we know about Jesus' life and the message he spoke. We will take a look at the impact Jesus had on the men who became his first disciples and how his message began to spread. Jesus' story as a man on Earth ends with his execution at the relatively young age of thirty-three. Despite the short time he was part of history, it was not the end of his legacy—it was just the beginning.

His teachings carried on through close friends like the apostles John and Peter and through evangelizers and writers like Luke, Paul, and Timothy, among many others. Their backgrounds, whom they wrote to, whom they spoke with, and why give insight into what was happening culturally and religiously during this time of great change.

Eventually, the Jewish world experienced great political upheaval and the catastrophic loss of their center of worship through the iron-like army of the Roman Empire. The budding Christian congregations were also affected by turmoil brought on by imperial rule. What was life like for early Christians? How did they become organized amidst such a chaotic political backdrop? How could they survive intense persecution and stay intact as one united entity?

Through the gospels and epistles, it is evident that Christianity was not just for men. They were not the only ones moved by Christian teachings, nor were they the only ones who faced the fire of persecution. Numerous women in the early Christian congregation are mentioned by name and noted for their faith and good deeds. What was the early Christian view of women, especially in comparison to the Jewish viewpoint? Who were some of the important women whose names are engraved in early Christian history?

This walk through early Christian history will give a glimpse not only of the first Christian congregations and their teachings but also the stories of eyewitness and those who experienced its birth and progression. It will also tell how things slowly began to evolve as the political scene changed.

Early Christianity left its mark on religion, worship, art, and culture. As a bonus, this book explores some early Christian artwork and their meanings and what we can learn about life and Christianity through the creativity of those who lived it.

Chapter 1: Origins and Background

The Jewish people had been in eager anticipation. The time they had been waiting for more than one thousand years—the appearance of the prophesied Messiah—was near at hand. Most were familiar with the words of the earlier prophets and understood the general timeline of events as laid out in prophetic writings. What did they know just before the birth of Jesus that led them to believe he would soon be born?

The Jews had not been left to guess who the Messiah would be through vague or confusing information. Although they did not know what his name would be, the Jewish writings [1] had hundreds of prophecies containing details that would help them identify the Messiah once he came. What were some of these?

Even those who did not believe Jesus was the one they were waiting for recognized certain facts about the Messiah, namely that he would have a royal lineage. He would be a descendant of King David of the tribe of Judah. The Hebrew prophecies were specific about the place he

---

[1] Most are included among the books of the Hebrew Scriptures (also known as the Old Testament). Books that contain prophecies about Jesus span multiple authors and periods and were written on scrolls during this period and prior. According to Alfred Edersheim in his book, *The Life and Times of Jesus the Messiah,* the Hebrew writings contain more than 400 prophecies about the coming Messiah. In fact, the entirety of the Hebrew Scriptures is in some way connected to the Messiah and is a virtual pathway toward his existence.

would be born—Bethlehem Ephrathah.[2] However, how would the Jews know *when* to expect this Messiah?

Prophets held in high regard by the Jewish people, like Daniel, provided a timeline of when the Messiah would appear. Daniel 9:25 (Rotherham) states: "From the going forth of the word to restore and rebuild Jerusalem" until the Messiah (literally meaning Anointed One) there would be sixty-nine weeks.[3] That "word" or royal decree was given by Persian King Artaxerxes Longimanus in 455 BCE when he allowed the exiled Jews to return and rebuild Jerusalem. What happened sixty-nine weeks after that decree? Nothing of significance.

However, the Encyclopedia Judaica states the understanding of the term "weeks" would actually be weeks of years (one "week" equaling seven years) a calculation method that was not uncommon for the Jews. By that calculation, seven times sixty-nine, the Jews arrived at 483 *years* from 455 BCE. Since there was no year zero, 483 years would bring the arrival of the Messiah to 29 AD. Did anything notable happen during that year? Yes, it was the year Jesus was baptized and began his ministry.

Though it doesn't appear the Jews knew the exact day, month, or year the one they were waiting for would come, they had a general idea and expected his arrival not long after the first quarter of the century. Right after Jesus' birth, Luke 2:38 says that the prophetess Anna told the event to "all the ones waiting for deliverance of Jerusalem."[4]

Why were the Jews, including historian Flavius Josephus, so eagerly waiting for deliverance, and from whom? The historical context gives us a clear view of the situation leading to the beginning of the first century.

Relationships with Greece and Rome

The mighty Alexander the Great was dead, and four of his generals had split his empire. Two generals, Antigonus and Ptolemy, split Judea down the middle. Although they did not have the same power as the

---

[2] During that time, two cities carried the name Bethlehem. One was in Zebulun. However, Micah 5:2 specifies that the Messiah would be born in the small town of Bethlehem Ephrathah in Judea, the same city King David was born in. Though there has been debate about Jesus' birthplace due to his being called a Nazarene, the designation was given because he was *raised* in the town of Nazareth.

[3] The Encyclopedia Judaica notes that there would be seventy weeks, but the "anointed prince" would be cut off, or killed, near the end of the seventieth week.

[4] The city of Jerusalem housed the temple and was the spiritual center of worship for the Jewish people, making it a place of high value and significance.

man who came before them, they continued his quest to spread Hellenism throughout the empire, which eventually knocked on the door of the Jews in Judea.

At least in the beginning, the Jews resented the Greeks and found pagan Greek culture abhorrent. In particular, the Greeks' large pantheon of colorful gods was vastly at odds with the Jewish belief in one Almighty God. The Greeks wore clothing that the Jews would have considered immodest, not to mention the nude wrestling and prevalence of homosexuality—violations of scriptural law. To have these influences thrust on them would make it more difficult to maintain the purity of their worship—a fundamental element of who they were.

But as Greek culture spread its fingers into Jerusalem and the surrounding area, Jews had a choice to make. Many chose the traditional route and kept themselves separate from pagan influences. Other Jews saw that the only way to get ahead and achieve elite status was to have a "when in Vegas" (or, in this case, Greece) philosophy—they learned Greek, gave their kids a Greek education, and became Hellenized to some extent. A schism formed between the two lines of thought, and in Jerusalem, a stir began over how much Hellenization was acceptable.

Many of the nobles and priests in Jerusalem favored adopting Greek culture more fully. In 175 BC, the High Priest Jason had a Greek-style gymnasium (a Greek center for education) and other Greek buildings built in the city.[5] He even paid the Seleucid ruler Antiochus Epiphanes (Antiochus IV) to officially label Jerusalem a Greek city. This was more than just advancement on his part; it was a power move. Establishing a gymnasium would tempt any prominent families who were against Hellenization. If they wanted to be educated and have their kids educated, it would have to be through a Greek educational system.

Antiochus IV also dangled Greek citizenship in front of the Jews—anyone who wanted the distinction and benefits of Greek citizenship must have a Greek education. For boys, that did not mean just academic learning but Greek military training.

Problems really began to heat up in 167 AD when a Jew named Menelaus tried to overthrow High Priest Jason and *buy* his way into the high priest position. Since Antiochus IV had the final say in appointing

---

[5] At this time, Jerusalem and the Jewish population did not have a political ruler, but the high priest was considered their spiritual and quasi-political leader.

the high priest, the position could go to the highest bidder. Short on funds, Menelaus looted gold from the temple in Jerusalem to get enough money to pay his way to being the high priest—an outrageous act that was viewed as stealing from God himself.[6]

Fighting broke out among Jewish factions and rioting ensued. The chaos became so great that Antiochus sent in the military—Syrian forces under Greek command marched into the city.

Radical changes began to take place. The temple was turned into Greco-Syrian barracks. This was another severe affront to faithful Jews, yet it was only the beginning. Circumcision, which was to be strictly observed according to the Mosaic Law, was banned. In fact, observance or even reading of the Torah, the first five books of the Bible containing Jewish laws, was now forbidden. Copies were searched out and burned.

Many Jews were compelled to hide their circumcision to appear more Greek. Others joined in pagan celebrations, adorning themselves with ivy and marching in a procession celebrating the Greek god of wine and debauchery, Dionysus. Some accounts say that a pig, an animal considered unclean under Mosaic Law, was sacrificed on the temple altar. As an additional insult, Antiochus IV had the most holy area of the temple turned into a center for pagan worship, a chamber rededicated to the Greek Zeus.

Until this time, the Greeks had left the Jews to follow their own laws uninhibited. The Jews had governed themselves and maintained and preserved their religious beliefs. But Antiochus IV did not like that the Jews felt accountable only to God and not a human ruler. He made more efforts to limit and or outright forbid Jewish religious practices, including the observance of the Sabbath and other sacred festivals. Many Jews felt that pagan Hellenistic ways were being forced onto them. They were also unable to govern themselves according to their laws and beliefs, and perhaps worst of all, the temple, their center of worship, was being grossly desecrated.

Some Jews believed this was all a pleasant mixing of cultures, perhaps thinking they were modernizing their culture. But to Jews faithful to their laws and beliefs, this was apostasy. Ultimately, these differences were the fuel for what became known as the Maccabean Revolt, launched by

---

[6] The temple in Jerusalem was the most important structure to the Jewish people, a representation of God's presence.

priest Mattathias and his sons.

When Greek officers accompanied by a Jewish priest came to the village where Mattathias lived, they tried to enforce a royal mandate that everyone make an offering to the gods. Although promised that this one act would earn him friendship with the king, Mattathias remained steadfast in his refusal to worship other gods. The Jewish people only worshipped one God, Yahweh.[7]

When another Jewish man complied and made the offering, a serious sin under Jewish law, Mattathias killed the man and one of the king's officers. Jews, Syrians, and Greeks now had a grievance with him—he had committed murder, which was against secular *and* Jewish law. So, he fled to the mountains with his sons. However, this was just the beginning of the uprising for Mattathias and his sons. It was the event that touched off the Maccabean Revolt.[8]

Mattathias and his sons did not remain alone in the hills—many followed them. From their location in the mountains, Mattathias and his sons gathered an army and began a campaign of guerilla warfare against the much more powerful Greco-Syrian army and Jews who had compromised their faith. It was as much a civil war among the Jews as it was a battle against the Greeks and the enforcement of Greek laws and pagan customs.

After a series of battles and the death of Mattathias in 166 BCE, the Jews, now under the command of Judas Maccabaeus, finally recaptured Jerusalem in December 164 BCE. Later that month, they rededicated the temple and cleansed it of all traces of pagan Greek worship, much to the celebration of the people.

A brief peace negotiated with the Syrian Greeks following the death of Antiochus IV gave both sides a break from the fighting—but it didn't last long. This time, the Jews turned to Rome for help, laying the groundwork for a situation akin to letting in the tiger to get rid of the wolf.

---

[7] From the original Hebrew letters YHWH, the Latinized translation of which is Jehovah.

[8] The family name was actually Hasmoneus. The moniker Maccabaeus or Maccabee was an honorary title later given to Mattathias' son Judah when he took leadership of the revolt after his father's death. He was perhaps given this title after scoring some decisive victories. The Maccabee name was later extended to include the entire family. Translations from Hebrew give possible meanings as "the hammer" or "the extinguisher."

However, for the next 100 years, the Jews regained control of Judea and ruled themselves. That was, until the fierce Roman General Pompey marched into Jerusalem in 63 BCE. By this time, the Roman Empire was on the rise, steadily conquering territories. However, Judea was still under Jewish leadership in Jerusalem. That leadership was fractured, with two factions headed by two brothers, Hyrcanus and Aristobulus, fighting a bloody war for control.

After accusations by Aristobulus against Pompey's Syrian representative, Pompey brought his troops down to Jerusalem to see what was happening. This gave Rome a dangerous foothold in the city. When he arrived, Pompey chose to side with Hyrcanus. After the Romans built a siege dam near the north wall, the incessant beat of battering rams and deluge of heavy stones from catapults finally broke through the walls, and the Roman army entered Jerusalem.

Like the Greeks before them, the Romans entered the temple and walked into the Holy of Holies—a place only the high priest could enter during certain times of the year. Though many Jews were killed by the Romans, many killed themselves rather than see the desecration of their temple again. Pompey set up Hyrcanus as the high priest and sole political leader of the nation. That was, until Julius Caesar appointed a regent, Antipater, to rule alongside Hyrcanus. After Hyrcanus became a prisoner of war in 40 BC, Antipater's son Herod (later known as Herod the Great) was set on the throne as the sole ruler of Judea.

That's not to say Rome gave up control of the area. Herod was put on the throne as a semi-independent vassal king of the Roman Empire. This began the Roman occupation that the Jews were oppressed by into the first century. Though Rome did not have a daily presence among the Jews, their domineering power could be felt in everyday life. For the most part, however, Rome allowed the Jews to live according to their customs and even made exceptions for them regarding certain mandates like military conscription.

Brilliant and ambitious, not to mention brutal, Herod wouldn't put up with any opposition from Jewish rebels discontented with him or Rome. However, he struck a good balance between keeping Rome happy and protecting the Jewish way of life. He even rebuilt the temple into an architectural marvel, making it somewhat of a tourist attraction for Jews and Gentiles alike. However, tensions with Rome and among the Jews continued to simmer.

Once Rome started appointing procurators over Judea around the start of the first century, things quickly slid downhill. Typically low-status officials in Rome, the procurators easily fell into corruption. The people often never saw the benefits of money designated for public projects. Instead, it was embezzled by officials who continued to grow richer. One of the most grievous cases was when Pontius Pilate needed to build a new aqueduct for the city's water supply. He stole money from the temple treasury to fund it, touching off a protest that ended in a Jewish slaughter.

Some Jewish zealots who believed in returning control of the land back to Jewish hands went further than protests. A rebel simply known as "The Egyptian" gathered 30,000 men in a failed attempt to take on the Roman army garrison in Jerusalem and install himself as ruler. Rome often swiftly came down on dissenters, whether minor protests or armed rebellions, with excessive and brutal force.

Roman taxes were a particularly prickly subject because the Jews were already suffering under an economic system that caused many small businesses and landowners to lose their livelihoods. More and more Jews went into poverty and debt. So, when procurators forced people to pay double the tax amount set by Rome so that they could keep the extra for themselves, the Jews were enraged.

While initially Rome had no issues with Jewish religious customs, contempt and intolerance of their practices crept in with the installation of procurators. The Roman historian Tacitus wrote that a certain Jewish ritual was "preposterous and morbid." Disrespect for long-held Jewish beliefs and customs made for an unfriendly atmosphere.

But it wasn't just the Romans who treated the Jews with contempt—so did their own religious leader. Calling the common people *am ha'aretz*, an insulting Hebrew term meaning "people of the land or dirt," the upper religious classes of the Pharisees and Sadducees began enslaving their own people with oppressive and rigid religious observances.

So, it was against this backdrop of more than 200 years of fighting, foreign domination, and religious oppression that the Jews were desperately looking for the promised savior. The Jewish Encyclopedia says, "They yearned for the promised deliverer of the house of David, who would free them from the yoke of the hated foreign usurper, would put an end to the impious Roman rule, and would establish His own reign of peace." The Jewish people believed salvation from their oppressor would be from God, but through a political entity that would restore their kingdom when he came. However, little did they realize that their expectations for the Messiah were not exactly in line with Jesus' broader purpose.

By the time Jesus came onto the scene, the Jewish province of Judea, ruled by Herod, was under the umbrella of the Roman Empire.

Chapter 2: The Gospels

Good news! This is the very meaning of the word "gospel." The four gospel accounts of Matthew, Mark, Luke, and John contain information about the life of Jesus and talk about the "good news" that he preached during his three-and-a-half-year ministry. Though none of the accounts are a comprehensive biography of Jesus' life, they tell certain details about his birth and childhood that would be especially important to the Jewish people in expectation of the fulfillment of prophecies regarding the Messiah. Not much is told about his childhood, teenage years, or young adulthood. Instead, the Gospels focus on Jesus' ministry and his teachings, telling of his purpose and laying the foundation for the first Christian congregations.

A Synopsis of the Gospels

Some might think that the Gospels are all the same, and to some extent, they are.[9] This is mainly because they or the eyewitnesses who related events to them, were seeing and hearing the same things. Yet the books are not the same because the people who wrote them were different—their backgrounds, education, occupations, relationships, and perspectives all varied. That affected how their Gospels were written and the details included. The details a physician might view as important to write down might not be the same as those a fisherman would zero in on. Although some of the stories overlap, they create a picture of the life

---

[9] The Gospels of Matthew, Mark, and Luke are often referred to as synoptic, or "like view," because of the similarities between the writings.

of Jesus. This is the account they tell.

In 3 BCE Nazareth, a young, unmarried, virgin woman named Mary was engaged to a Jewish carpenter named Joseph. Though she was a very faithful Jewish woman, she was still surprised to be visited at her home by an angel named Gabriel, appearing as a man. He announced he had good news to tell her. But Mary was not the first person Gabriel appeared to with stunning news.

A few months earlier, he had appeared to an older Jewish priest named Zechariah, a man whose wife was a relative of Mary's. Shockingly, he told Zechariah that his wife, Elizabeth, would have a son. Zechariah was in disbelief—his wife was too old to have children! Not long after, Elizabeth became pregnant. She gave birth to a son named John, who became known as John the Baptizer (or Baptist).

That same angel told Mary something she found just as astonishing: that, although she was a virgin, she would give birth to a son. Stunned, she asked how that was possible. Gabriel told her it would be with the help of God's holy spirit, and the child would be God's son.[10] Mary was somewhat skeptical, but to prove that what he said was possible, he told her about the unlikely pregnancy of her relative, Elizabeth.

Shortly after the angel left Mary, she visited Elizabeth and found that her older relative was pregnant as Gabriel said. When Elizabeth found out about Mary's pregnancy, she exclaimed that the younger woman was truly blessed. But Mary knew that when she went home and it became obvious she was pregnant, not everyone would feel the same way. In fact, she could be in real trouble.

Mary had valid feelings of worry—how would she explain her pregnancy to her family, let alone her fiancé? Not only that, but according to Jewish law, a married or engaged woman who willingly had a sexual relationship with another man would be given a death sentence.

It had been three months since she had seen Joseph, and she had a lot to tell him. She confided to him what happened; unsurprisingly, he found it hard to believe. He went away very grieved, wondering what he

---

[10] The Bible uses the Hebrew word *ru'ach* and the Greek word *pneu'ma* for spirit, both of which mean "breath" or "wind," symbolic of life energy or life force. Second-century Christian Justin Martyr explained the Holy Spirit (*pneu'ma hagion*) as the "influence or mode of operation of the Deity." Simply put, he was saying it was the energy or force God used to do things (like creating). Therefore, some Bible translations also use the term "God's active force" when referring to the Holy Spirit.

should do. He knew Mary was a good woman and loved her, but he couldn't see any other way she could be pregnant except by another man. Still, he didn't want Mary to die in disgrace. So, he considered secretly divorcing her.[11]

When he went to sleep one night, an angel appeared to him in a dream and confirmed what Mary had told him. Following the angel's instructions, he went ahead and married Mary. A few months later, while Mary was heavily pregnant, a census decreed by Roman emperor Augustus Caesar required Joseph and Mary to return to Bethlehem, the city of Joseph's birth, to participate in the registry.[12] When they got to Bethlehem, it was so crowded with travelers that the couple had nowhere to stay except a stable. It was there in the hay, surrounded by stable animals, that Mary gave birth to a son, Jesus. She wrapped him in some pieces of cloth and laid him in a manger, or trough, used for animal feed.

In the fields outside the city that night, some Jewish shepherds were suddenly surrounded by a bright light.[13] An angel appeared before them and told them there was good news: the savior they were waiting for had been born. The angel also told them where to find him—a stable in Bethlehem. Before they could leave, other angels appeared and sang with joy, "Glory in the heights above to God, and upon earth peace among men of goodwill."

The shepherds wasted no time rushing to Bethlehem to find Jesus. When they did, they told Mary and others in Bethlehem about the angel

---

[11] Mary and Joseph were only engaged at the time, but in ancient Jewish culture, an engagement was binding and would need a divorce to break it off.

[12] Census registrations were common in ancient history. There were several recorded during the reign of Augustus Caesar. According to fourth-century historian Orosius, this census, recorded by Luke as taking place in 2 BCE, may have been the event where all the nations under the Roman Empire swore an oath of loyalty to Caesar to unite them as one society.

[13] Though tradition holds that Jesus was born on December 25th, the Gospels do not say when he was born. In that region, December is typically a cold, rainy (and sometimes snowy) month, so shepherds would not have been outdoors with their flocks. It is also unlikely that Joseph, Mary, and others would have traveled for a census in that weather or that Caesar would have required a winter journey of people already on the verge of rebellion. The Catholic Encyclopedia says that "the celebration of Christmas is of Roman origin and dates from around 330 AD ... It had been customary for Roman pagans to gather at Vatican Hill to worship deities of the east, the choice of December 25..." Some details in the Gospels point to Jesus being born around late September or early October, yet there is no record or evidence of early first-century Christians celebrating the birth of Christ.

and what was said to them.

To complete Jewish rituals surrounding the birth of a baby, Joseph and Mary stayed in Bethlehem for over a month. In the meantime, foreign astrologers saw a strange sight in the night sky—a new star that had never appeared before.[14] It led them to Jerusalem, where they visited King Herod the Great. They told him they had followed a strange new star to Jerusalem and were going to Bethlehem to see "the one born king of the Jews" and pay their respects. Herod, who tolerated no rivalry for his position, was disconcerted by this "king of the Jews" report. Pretending that he, too, wanted to pay his respects, Herod told the astrologers to report back once they found him.

The astrologers left and again followed the star right to the house where Joseph and Mary were staying and brought their gifts. When they were about to return to tell Herod, they were given a divine warning in a dream not to do so because Herod actually wanted to kill the child. They decided to avoid Herod altogether by going home another way.

Angered that he hadn't been told where Jesus was, Herod took drastic and unthinkable action—he gave an order to kill all baby boys two years old and younger in and around Bethlehem.[15] To save Jesus' life, an angel appeared to Joseph and told them they must flee to Egypt as quickly as possible. The three escaped just in time. After Herod the Great died, an angel again appeared to Joseph and told him it was safe to return home. They returned to Judea and settled in Nazareth, avoiding the sphere of Herod's unpopular son, Archelaus, who was now the ruler

---

[14] The original Greek word used here is magi (plural form), which most people use and recognize. Magi (singular magos) is sometimes translated as sorcerer, conjurer, or in this instance, astrologer. Given the men's knowledge of the stars, astrologer appears to be a logical translation. Though traditionally it is said there were three magi, none of the Gospels state the exact number that visited Herod or Mary and Jesus. The book of Matthew says they came from the east, likely Persia/Babylon.

[15] There are no contemporary secular records of Herod's massacre of the babies, but there is historical context for the event. Herod went down in history for being ruthless and brutal. Bent on keeping his throne and tolerating no hint of rivalry, he had forty-five men murdered for supporting a potential rival. He even had his closest friends and family members executed, including three of his sons, his beloved second wife, her brother, her grandfather, and many others. In the eyes of historians, this makes it highly plausible that Herod would murder a group of young children in an attempt to wipe out a "king of the Jews" who might have been born and could become a potential threat to his rulership. Also, Roman writer Macrobius (ca 400 AD) wrote in his book *Saturnalia* that he had heard about the incident.

of the province. There, Jesus grew up as a carpenter's son.[16][17]

The Gospels don't detail Jesus' life growing up, except for one incident when he was twelve. Luke details a time when the family was traveling back home from Passover celebrations in Jerusalem with a large group of family and friends. Believing that Jesus was among the group, Joseph and Mary did not realize he was not with them until the next day. Returning to Jerusalem to look for him, they found him at the temple with the Jewish religious leaders, asking questions and listening to them speak.

Mary, quite frazzled and distressed, asked her son why he would do this to her. He replied, "Did you not know I would be in the house of my Father?"

From there, it is seventeen years before Jesus' story picks up again. Matthew and Luke record Jesus' early years, giving context to his life (and, in Matthew, proof that Jesus was fulfilling prophecies about the Messiah). However, Mark and John start their accounts before and during Jesus' ministry—something they wanted to highlight. Within Christendom, there is often much focus on Jesus' birth and death, but all four Gospels emphasize Jesus' ministry and purpose.

All four gospel writers also spend time detailing the ministry of John the Baptizer, whose work was to prepare the Jewish people to accept the Messiah.

In the spring of 29 AD, the region around the Jordan River was abuzz with talk of a man who wore a camel hair shirt and leather girdle. He lived in the wilderness, eating honey and locusts. He was also a relative of Jesus (the son of Mary's cousin Elizabeth). But it was his message that stirred people the most. He told the Jewish people, "Repent, for the kingdom of the heavens has drawn near." He began baptizing people as a symbol of their repentance.

Six months into John's ministry, Jesus, now thirty, went to see him. John baptized his relative in the Jordan River to set an example for the disciples that would follow. John the Baptizer put Jesus under the water, and when Jesus came up, Matthew, Luke, and John (an eyewitness to the

---

[16] Based on Josephus' history and chronology, Herod died around 4 or 5 AD. With the threat removed, Joseph and Mary could safely return to Judea with their young son.

[17] Some Bible scholars believe that Jesus' parable of the minas recorded in Luke 19 might have been inspired by Archelaus.

event) all say that God's holy spirit appeared in the form of a dove. A voice was heard from heaven saying, "You are my Son, the beloved; I have approved you."

This was a pivotal moment in Jesus' life because it touched off his ministry and, according to some gospel teachings, was when he officially became the Messiah.

Matthew, Mark, and Luke record that right afterward, Jesus was tempted three times by Satan (the devil) in the wilderness. In his last audacious attempt, Satan offered Jesus the power and prestige of ruling the world's governments if Jesus would just agree to bow down in one act of worship. Jesus denied all three of Satan's attempts and firmly told him, "Go away!"

Not long after, some of John the Baptizer's disciples believed that he was the Messiah. The first of these were Andrew and his brother, Peter. A few days later, they, along with Jesus and other new disciples John, Philip, Nathanael, and possibly James, went to a wedding celebration in Cana. When John wrote about this, it wasn't a diary of a social gathering but a recounting of Jesus' first miracle—turning large jars of water into very good wine.

Not long after that, in the spring of 30 AD, Jesus and some of his disciples went to celebrate the Passover in Jerusalem. When they got to the temple, what Jesus saw filled him with righteous indignation. Merchants were exploiting people by overcharging for sacrificial animals and exchanging foreign money.

He braided together some rope into a whip and used it to chase the crooked merchants away, overturning their tables in disgust. He told them, "Get these (things) away from here; do not make my Father's house a market."

Later, when Jesus was traveling to Galilee, he went to get water from Jacob's well near Sychar (modern day Nablus). There, he met a Samaritan woman. Asking her for water led to a poignant conversation where he revealed he knew her tainted social background and the bias against her for it. During this conversation, the unnamed woman became the first person Jesus outright told that he was the Messiah.[18] She went off

---

[18] This is historically and culturally significant for a few reasons. First, during this time, women were treated like second-class citizens, even in Jewish society. Jewish men would never be seen in public talking to women who weren't relatives. Secondly, Jews and Samaritans generally hated

and told others in the city. Word got around, motivating many to become followers of Jesus.

As he traveled, Jesus performed various miracles. He said they served a purpose besides just helping those who needed it. When an official in the court of Herod Antipas found out that Jesus was in Capernaum, he rushed to meet him. He asked Jesus to help his son, who was sick and about to die. Jesus told the man that he would perform miracles because "unless you people see signs and wonders, you will never believe." He informed the official that his son was, in fact, now alive and well. When the official returned home, his servants told him his son was healed in the hour Jesus said.

It was not the only healing recorded by the Gospel writers. They also record him healing many who were sick or had disabilities, including a completely paralyzed man, lepers, a blind man, people with chronic illnesses, and the apostle Peter's mother-in-law.[19] He even expelled demons from those afflicted by possession. On one Sabbath day, he healed a man with a withered hand, something that shocked and angered the Pharisees, who interpreted this as forbidden "work" on the Sabbath day[20]. This attracted their attention negatively, and from then on, they were on the lookout for ways to discredit or even kill him.

Even though many flocked to Jesus because of his miracles and sermons, some took offense at the truths he spoke. In one instance, he referenced a prior historical situation and applied it to the selfishness and faithlessness of the Jewish people as a whole. This made the crowd in the synagogue violently angry, and they pushed Jesus out of the city and to the top of a mountain. At the top, they tried to throw him over a ledge headfirst. However, Luke says that Jesus escaped the harrowing incident by walking right out of the crowd.

Later, after Jesus chose twelve apostles, the thirteen men were sitting

---

each other and had very deep-seated prejudices. This was an example of Jesus' respect for women and lack of prejudice based on gender or race.

[19] Leprosy was a terrible disease that could leave a person severely disfigured or even lead to death. It was very contagious, and according to Jewish law, no one was to touch a leper. Someone with leprosy was not to go near other people without calling out to warn them. So, it is notable that the Gospels mention incidents of Jesus touching lepers to heal them, even though he healed others without using touch. The Gospels say this was purposeful, as Jesus felt pity for them and recognized their emotional need for human contact.

[20] Pharisees were highly educated Jewish religious leaders who often added to and enforced Jewish law.

on the Mount of Olives.[21] They were tired and trying to rest, but people from miles away had gathered to see Jesus. A large crowd formed on the hillside, hoping to get healed or hear him speak. Although exhausted, Jesus did not want to disappoint those who had come. All those in the crowd who came to be healed, he healed. Against this backdrop, Jesus gave one of the most famous speeches in history—the Sermon on the Mount.

The sermon, which Matthew records in lengthy detail throughout three chapters, hits on many subjects. Throughout, Jesus talked about how to gain happiness, control anger, the benefits of spiritual thinking and living, the trap of materialism, and how to deal with being offended. He condemned hypocrisy and emphasized the importance of showing love to others. He also taught the dangers of being overly critical towards others, gave an example of how to pray, highlighted the reasons for trusting in God, and told his disciples that their actions, not just empty words, would prove who they really were. Perhaps the most well-known of his points is what many now call "The Golden Rule" in Matthew 7:12: "All things, therefore, that you want men to do to you, you must likewise do to them."[22]

Matthew, Mark, and Luke record the crowd's reaction to the sermon—the people were "astounded" by his words. This is mentioned several times in the Gospels. Jesus often used thought-provoking questions and easy-to-understand stories and illustrations in his teaching method. He became renowned for his talent as a teacher.

Later, Jesus and some of his disciples found themselves in a frightening situation. One night, they took a wooden boat and crossed the Sea of Galilee.[23] In the dark, a sudden and fierce storm whipped up across the waters.[24] While the storm raged, Jesus slept peacefully on a pillow at the stern of the boat. Even though the disciples were experienced fishermen and had undoubtedly weathered storms before,

---

[21] The Greek word for apostle means "someone sent by another" or "a messenger." Even though the term is sometimes loosely applied to many or all of Jesus' disciples, in this context it is the twelve disciples specially selected as representatives.

[22] This verse is often quoted as "Do unto others as you would have them do to you."

[23] Sometimes referred to as the "Sea of Galilee Boat" or the "Jesus Boat," these common ancient fishing vessels were typically around twenty-seven feet long, 7.5 feet wide, and 4.3 feet high.

[24] Though often mild, the Sea of Galilee is occasionally battered by sudden and intense storms with dramatic waves (up to ten feet, as recorded in 1992) that could swamp a smaller boat.

they had trouble controlling the boat and started to fear for their lives. They woke Jesus and desperately asked him, "Don't you care that we are about to die?!"

Jesus got up calmly and called out to the storm, "Peace! Be still!" The storm immediately died down. The disciples were so amazed by the miracle that they fearfully asked each other, "Who is this that even the wind and the sea obey him?"

Sea of Galilee boat.
Travellers & Tinkers, CC BY-SA 4.0 <https://creativecommons.org/licenses/by-sa/4.0>, via Wikimedia Commons; https://commons.wikimedia.org/wiki/File:JesusBoat.jpg

The incident with the storm did not deter Jesus or the others from getting back in a boat and going onto the Sea of Galilee again. But this time, all four Gospel writers recorded a different type of miracle. To get a break from the crowds, Jesus and his disciples crossed the water to go to a more isolated location. However, the crowds followed, and Jesus felt bad that they had traveled a long way to get healed and hear him speak and were now hungry. It was late in the day and nearly impossible to get food for the almost 10,000 people there. This is the scenario behind one of Jesus' most well-known miracles—feeding thousands with just five loaves of bread and two small fish. He and his disciples broke up the food and distributed it. No one went hungry, and in fact, there were twelve baskets of leftovers.

Between the healing, the food, the sermons, and other miracles, many Jewish people were convinced that Jesus was the savior they had been hoping for and tried to make him their king. He refused, time and again emphasizing that God's heavenly kingdom was the only solution to their problems. But it was not the answer they expected. The people were confused. Many stopped following him because they believed he was sent to be their ruler and rescue them from oppression right then. Many questioned whether he was really the Messiah of prophecy.

The religious leaders—the Pharisees, in particular—didn't like Jesus, especially because, on more than one occasion, he condemned their oppression and contempt for the common people. He butted heads with them many times, and they decided they needed to get rid of him. They looked for reasons to have him arrested, but Jesus slipped through their fingers every time. On one occasion, they even tried to grab him and stone him to death for blasphemy, but he again escaped their grasp.

Jesus went north to escape the mob, but it was then he received devastating news: his good friend Lazarus had fallen sick and died. However, there was a bit of an issue. Going to see Lazarus' family would mean going back to Judea where the people wanted to kill him. But his disciples were on board with going, and together they headed toward the village of Bethany, where Lazarus' sisters Martha and Mary lived.

When he got there and saw the sisters crying, he was overcome with empathetic grief and cried with them. Lazarus' body was in a cave with a large boulder covering the entrance. Everyone went to the tomb to mourn. Jesus told some men to move the boulder, but Martha objected, and for good reason. She said, "He has been here four days; his body must smell by now!"

Jesus reassured her it would be okay. He prayed out loud in front of everyone and called into the tomb, "Lazarus, come out!" To everyone's astonishment, Lazarus, bound in his funeral cloth, walked out of the cave. They unwrapped him so he could be reunited with family and friends.

When word of the resurrection got out, more high-ranking religious leaders plotted his death. Jesus again eluded them for the time being.

In early spring, he went up to Jerusalem just before Passover. It was then that he foretold something truly disturbing to the Jews—the future destruction of their beloved holy city.[25] This did nothing to quell the murderous rage of the Jewish religious leaders, but they had to tread carefully because many people believed he was a prophet. So, instead of an all-out violent encounter, they tried to trick him with a question about taxes, hoping he would say something they could claim was seditious. Jesus didn't fall for it, and their plan failed again. However, despite escaping time and again, Jesus knew his death was approaching and made reference to it before sharing some of his final teachings.

On the day of Nisan 12, Jesus was lying low because he knew there was a plot brewing against him. Meanwhile, the religious leaders who wanted to kill him were practically handed the tool to do it: one of Jesus' apostles, Judas Iscariot, agreed to betray Jesus to them for thirty pieces of silver (the typical price for a slave)

While the other disciples prepared for the Passover, it seems Jesus was already suspicious of Judas and didn't give him any details that might allow him to interrupt their Passover celebration.

During the Passover meal, Jesus told his disciples this would be his last meal with them. He then got a towel and washed their feet to set an example of love and hospitality.[26] Afterward, he made a shocking announcement: "One of you will betray me." The apostles were stunned by the revelation. Yet Jesus did not outright say who it was. Instead, he told Judas to leave and do what he needed to do. When Judas left, Jesus told his apostles that he was instituting a new commemoration for his followers instead of the Passover.

After a heart-to-heart talk with the men, he warned them that things would not be easy going forward. In fact, they could expect sometimes violent opposition and persecution. With that in mind, he reminded them of their need for strong faith and careful obedience to what he had taught them. Jesus reassured them that God's holy spirit would be given to them to help them once he was gone. He prayed with and for them before they got up to leave around midnight.

When they left, the men went to the Garden of Gethsemane for a while. There, a mob including soldiers, the high priest, and others

---

[25] The destruction he was alluding to happened thirty-seven years later when the Romans, under General Titus, besieged and destroyed the city.

[26] An ancient Middle Eastern tradition usually performed by a host because travelers got dust on their feet while walking on unpaved roads with sandals.

approached Jesus, carrying weapons and torches. The man leading the crowd? Judas Iscariot. He approached Jesus and kissed his cheek. It was not a sign of affection but a predetermined signal to identify Jesus to the men who would arrest him.

Peter, in a characteristically impulsive moment, took a sword and cut off the ear of the high priest's servant. Healing it, Jesus told Peter to put the sword away because "all those that take up the sword will perish by the sword." Afterward, Jesus was taken into custody, and all but one of his disciples ran from the garden.

Jesus was eventually subjected to a trial in front of Pontius Pilate, the prefect of Judea, who found him innocent of any crimes. Yet the Jewish religious leaders incited the people to hatred. They demanded that he be sentenced to death, even after Pilate gave the crowd a choice to release Jesus or a murderer named Barabbas.

Feeling like he had no choice but to give in to the wishes of the crowd or risk his own position, Pilate symbolically washed his hands of the matter and had Jesus whipped with a scourge.[27] Afterward, the soldiers spit on him, slapped him, mocked him, and shoved a crown made of thorns onto his head. His dignity in the face of the abuse impressed Pilate, who then presented a beaten Jesus to the crowd to evoke pity. However, the crowd was determined.

On Nisan 14, after an agonizing day, Jesus and others slated for execution carried the large wooden stakes that they were to be hung on.[28] Jesus, thoroughly exhausted, collapsed. The Romans grabbed a man from the crowd, Simon of Cyrene, and compelled him to carry the stake for Jesus. The grim procession finally stopped at a location fittingly called Golgotha or "Skull Place."

---

[27] A small whip of several strips of leather intertwined with iron or animal bone, constructed to tear the flesh on contact.

[28] Although traditionally many English Bibles use the word cross, the original Greek word used was *stauros*. According to the Imperial Bible Dictionary, the word meant an "upright pole...on which anything might be hung." The Roman usage of the word *crux* (translated as "cross" in English) also originally indicated an "upright pole." The Catholic Encyclopedia says, "Certain it is, at any rate, that the cross originally consisted of a simple vertical pole, sharpened at its upper end." Sticking to that, some Bible translations use the word "stake" or "tree" instead of "cross." Some Bible writers also used the Greek word *xylon*, meaning a piece of timber or tree, instead of *stauros*. Because of this, certain Bible translations, like the Jerusalem Bible, use the word "tree" in this context.

Jesus and two criminals with him had their hands and feet nailed to the poles, which were then placed upright in the ground. Jesus' mother, Mary, was among those in the crowd watching the execution. Understandably, Mary would have felt as if her own body were being pierced with a sword.

At the moment Jesus died, a huge earthquake shook the area around Jerusalem, even damaging the temple. The Roman army officers and people in the crowd became afraid. The army officer in charge was moved to exclaim, "Certainly this was God's son!"

A member of the Sanhedrin (the Jewish high court) against the execution of Jesus was present when he died. He asked for the body and had it taken to be entombed. Two days later, several female disciples went to the tomb to properly treat the body with spices. They were shocked by what they found.

The large, heavy stone covering the entrance to the tomb had been moved, and the cave was empty. Jesus' body was missing. They ran off to tell Peter and some of the other disciples while Mary Magdalene stayed behind. Crying, she was approached by a caretaker who asked what is wrong. It took her a moment, but she suddenly recognized the man speaking to her—it was Jesus!

In the following days and weeks, hundreds of other disciples also saw and spoke to the resurrected Jesus. Some, like Thomas, had a hard time believing at first. But Jesus gave evidence through miracles that he was who he said he was.

Luke recounts both in the gospel he wrote and in the book of Acts that, after spending time with the apostles and disciples, giving them some last instructions and assurances, Jesus ascended to heaven in front of the apostles with no public fanfare.

Taken as a whole, the four books make a more complete account of Jesus' life and ministry. But what do we know about the men who wrote the Gospels and their original writings?

Matthew

Matthew was loathed by his own people because of his profession; some even considered what he did traitorous. He was a tax collector. To his fellow Jews, tax collectors were nothing more than an irritating thorn, a constant reminder that the Romans were their imperial overlords. Tax collectors were often viewed as sinners, largely because many of them dishonestly demanded more money than required to skim some for themselves. Most Jews considered tax collectors low class and avoided any voluntary association with them.

Matthew wrote his take on events through the lens of his profession. As a tax collector, it is no surprise that he mentions details relating to money and numbers. Likely treated to insults and contempt by his fellow countrymen, he emphasized Jesus' kindness, as reflected in the words he chose to record in Matthew 11:28-30: "Come to me all you who are toiling and loaded down, and I will refresh you...I am mild-tempered and lowly in heart and you will find refreshment for yourselves." Though his fellow Jews despised him for his profession, Matthew found a refreshing difference in how Jesus treated him and others. He enjoyed a close friendship with Jesus and became one of his first apostles. Matthew wrote numerous times regarding mercy, a quality he probably valued very highly.

Matthew wrote the book that bears his name in Palestine, his writings covering the years 2 BC to 33 AD. Although the exact year it was completed is not firmly known, later manuscripts date it to 41 AD. Nowhere in the book does Matthew mention himself as the writer, yet the unanimous belief that he penned it has been unwavering since the second century AD. Early Christians such as Papias, who was a contemporary or very nearly a contemporary of the apostle, attest to Matthew's authorship.

Looking into the language he wrote his original work in, the main objective of his writing, who he was primarily writing to, and the historical context make even more sense of the contents. Fourth-century Greek historian of Christianity Eusebius and fourth/fifth-century Christian scholar Jerome both repeatedly say that Matthew wrote the original manuscript "in his native tongue," Hebrew (later translated into Greek for non-Jews) Jerome backed this up by confirming that there was a Hebrew language copy in a library collection in Caesarea during his day. Since Matthew was in Palestine and his target audience was primarily Jews, it is logical that he would write in their language.

Right from the start, Matthew gets to the heart of his matter—proving to the Jewish people that Jesus is the promised Messiah they have been waiting for. He starts by tracing Jesus' lineage to Abraham, knowing its legal and prophetic importance would not be lost on faithful Jews. His very first words outline Jesus' lineage through Mary, tracing him back to

King David of the Israelite tribe of Judah.[29] He then gives a detailed account of the events surrounding Jesus' birth and childhood, presenting unique details not found anywhere else.

Matthew's logical way of thinking is seen in the order in which he writes events. The Gospel is not written chronologically as if it were a journal. Although he writes chronologically where it makes sense or is necessary, he groups Jesus' sermons and parables in topical order, emphasizing key teachings. He writes with the detailed precision one would expect from a man who served in a job that required precision and accuracy.

Mark

On the night Jesus was arrested, a certain young man was among his disciples, having apparently rushed out to the Garden of Gethsemane wearing nothing but an outer coat. He had either heard that Jesus and the apostles had gone to the garden and rushed out to follow or heard about the arrest in progress. All the rest with Jesus that night scattered and fled when the soldiers took him, but one stayed behind. Following Jesus nearby, he was soon spotted. When he was recognized as someone associated with Jesus, the soldiers and chief priests attempted to capture him, too. They grabbed onto his outer garment, but he managed to escape by wriggling out of his clothing running away completely naked.

John Mark (Roman Marcus, his surname), the writer of the Gospel of Mark, is the only one who mentions this young man, likely a firsthand account of his own harrowing escape. Mark was not an apostle, and he implies that he was still young around the time of Jesus' arrest. Mark packs a lot of action into his account of Jesus, some of it as an eyewitness but much of it as a recorder of the apostle Peter's eyewitness account. Second-century Christian scholars like Origen, Papias, and Tertullian attest that Mark wrote his gospel "in accordance with Peter's instructions" and confirmed that Mark was Peter's interpreter. Mark traveled with Peter and had a close relationship with the older apostle. Peter even referred to John Mark as "my son."

Even though Mark's telling of events closely mirrors Matthew's, some unique details and perspectives reflect Peter's influence—for example, when he writes about the terrible storm that rose up on the Sea of

---

[29] According to Jewish prophecies in the Old Testament/Hebrew Scriptures, the Messiah would come through the line of Judah.

Galilee. In his telling, Mark takes the time to mention seemingly insignificant details, such as the fact that Jesus was sleeping on the stern of the boat and using a pillow. These are things that a fisherman such as Peter might take note of.

The storm on the sea of Galilee is just one example of the fast-moving style and content included in Mark, another reflection of the emotional, impulsive, and very observant Peter. But in the details, we can also see that, although Mark was only an earwitness to some of the things he wrote, he was meticulous about accuracy. Eusebius said that "he gave attention, to leave out nothing of what he had heard and to make no false statements in them."

The shortest of the Gospels, Mark doesn't start at the beginning of Jesus' life but instead picks up at the beginning of Jesus' ministry and covers events over the years 29-33 AD. Mark wrote his account around 60-65 AD. He was in Rome at the time, and his target audience was Romans, apparent by the way he explains Jewish customs, culture, and other things that would not be familiar to non-Jews.

However, the gospel account is not where Mark's story ends. He reappears in the book of Acts alongside Paul, in one case as the subject of the older man's most heated incident on record.

Luke

Although Luke is referred to as an evangelist, that was not his first profession. The highly educated man was not an apostle, either. He was a physician, a fact that is reflected in his expansive vocabulary and detailed writing about those who suffered physical ailments—something he would naturally take notice of.

Luke also starts at the beginning of Jesus' story and covers the same years as Matthew—3 BC to 33 AD. He begins in chronological order, but after Jesus begins his ministry, Luke sometimes strays from linear writing and tells certain events and teachings by topic instead. For instance, while Matthew puts Jesus' family tree first, Luke doesn't list it until the third chapter, talking about it in terms of how Jesus' lineage through Joseph was recognized by the Jews at the time of his baptism.

Luke, not an eyewitness to the events he wrote about, interviewed many who were present to compile his writing. Even though his book comes third among the Gospels, Luke wrote it in 56-58 AD, between the time Matthew and Mark wrote theirs. Whereas they wrote to specific groups of people, Luke wrote for anyone who wanted to listen.

Like Mark, Luke's story doesn't end with his Gospel. He also traveled on missionary tours with Paul and is generally accepted as the writer of the action-packed account of the apostles and other first-century Christians in the book of Acts.[30]

John

Filled with fiery zeal and at one time asking if they could call down fire from heaven in vengeance, John and his brother James were labeled "Sons of Thunder" by Jesus.[31] It is interesting to see through John's writings how this dynamic apostle matured and accepted Jesus' teachings, later writing extensively about love.

Likely Jesus' cousin through Mary's sister Salome, John is said to be the apostle with the closest friendship with Jesus. In fact, while Jesus was on the stake dying, he entrusted his mother, likely by then a widow, to John's care.

A fisherman, he and Peter were disparaged as "plain illiterate men" by religious leaders who heard them preach. However, John proved them so very wrong. Far from illiterate, he wrote four books of the Bible besides the Gospel that bears his name.

When he wrote his gospel near the city of Ephesus in 98 AD, John was the last living apostle. He gives the most intimate picture of Jesus and who he was—and the most unique. Only 10 percent of what he covers is mentioned by the other Gospel writers.

In John 20:31, the apostle tells why he wrote his Gospel, saying these things were "written down so that you may believe that Jesus is the Christ, the Son of God" and so that readers "may have life by means of his name."

The accuracy of the four Gospels, Matthew, Mark, Luke, and John, has been confirmed by the writers themselves, those who knew them, and other early Christians who came later. However, there are books that touch on Jesus' life that did not make it into the Bible canon. What were they, and why were they left out?

---

[30] Luke is confirmed as the author as far back as second-century writers Irenaeus and Clement of Alexandria and according to the Muratorian Fragment, which is believed to have been written around 170 AD.

[31] Jesus quickly corrected the overzealous men and told them that would not be a proper response to the situation.

Apocryphal Books

The four included in the Bible are considered the only divinely-inspired Gospels. However, after these were written, "gospels" of a more fanciful nature began to turn up in writings and oral stories – about thirty of which are known. These have been called "apocryphal," an interesting term from the Greek language that translates as "to hide away." What was alleged to be hidden?

Some claimed to have a greater insider knowledge of Jesus and his teachings—things no one else knew about. For instance, the "Infancy Gospel of Thomas" talks about Jesus' life as a child, portraying him as more of a supernatural Dennis the Menace than the future Messiah. In this work, Jesus used his miraculous powers for mischief and vengeance. Instead of using his power to heal and resurrect the dead, the gospel claims that, as a child, he used it to maim and kill.

In the Gospel of Mary, the title character is the woman most loved by Jesus, who is given special teachings and understandings that she later shares with the apostles and disciples.[32] At one point, she is said to have confronted the apostle Peter over leadership and authority in the congregation.

Other apocryphal books, such as the Gospel of Judas and the Gospel of Peter, attempt to turn villains into heroes and vice versa. Judas' betrayal of Jesus is portrayed as nothing short of heroic, as the book claims he knew the real Jesus better than anyone. In one instance, it tells of a time when Jesus mocked his apostles over a lack of knowledge. In the Gospel of Peter, the writer exonerates Pontius Pilate from any responsibility over Jesus' death.

Many apocryphal books contain writings that experts consider more legend than fact and contradict what is written in the Bible Gospels. For instance, The Birth of Mary presents the idea that although Jesus' mother Mary married Joseph, she remained a virgin for the rest of her life.[33]

So, what are the differences between the Gospels included in the Bible and those that weren't? The biblical Gospels were written by those who knew Jesus or his apostles and were firsthand accounts from their

---

[32] There are questions among scholars about which biblical Mary this refers to, but many believe it to be Mary Magdalene. Most scholars consider this to be a Gnostic text.

[33] The Gospels mention other sons of Mary, Jesus' brothers.

own viewpoints or those who witnessed events. The non-canonical accounts were written by people who never personally knew Jesus or his apostles and often make bold claims that they reveal hidden truths about Jesus. Much of what is written in these is considered to be dubious or outright historical fiction.

Bible scholars have found no real evidence to question the authenticity of the inspired Gospels. But in contrast, Irenaeus, a professed Christian writer of the late second century, wrote that these apocryphal books were the works of apostates that "they themselves have forged, to bewilder the minds of foolish men."

After the biblical Gospels about Jesus ended, what then? After his death, what happened to Jesus' apostles and the work he started?

Chapter 3: The Apostles' Missions

With Judas' betrayal of Jesus and subsequent suicide, there was a spot left to fill among the apostles. However, that spot was not filled by Paul but by Matthias. In fact, Paul was not an original apostle (though he is often labeled as one), and he would not show up on the scene until later.

The apostles spear-headed and joined in the ministry work, performing miracles and spreading the "good news" in the temple and "from house to house." However, persecution of what was viewed as a new sect was just beginning to rear its violent head.

One of the fiercest persecutors of Jesus' disciples was a Pharisee named Saul. However, on his way to persecute Jesus' disciples in Damascus, Syria, he had a life-changing experience.

Seeing an extraordinarily bright light flash from the sky, Saul was rendered blind. A voice from heaven asked him, "Why are you persecuting me?" The voice then instructed him what to do next. This voice is identified in the book of Acts as none other than Jesus, now returned to heaven. To his own benefit, Saul decided to follow the instructions, leading to him being healed by a man named Ananias. When Saul regained his sight, he still went to Damascus, but this time, to preach about Jesus instead of persecute.

Things did not go well in Damascus, and Saul fled to Jerusalem. But once there, his reception by the disciples in the city was less than warm—Saul's reputation had preceded him. The disciples had a hard time believing that Saul had made such a drastic and complete turnaround and worried he was there to set a trap for them. However, a kind disciple named Barnabas jumped to Saul's defense and explained to the apostles and others how such an immense change had occurred for Saul.[34]

When word got back to Jerusalem that preaching to the Greeks in the Syrian city of Antioch had good results, Barnabas took Saul to Antioch. There, they found a "considerable crowd," and their work helped continue "adding to the Lord."

This was a very key year in the history of Christianity. The disciples in Antioch assembled over the next year, listening to the teachings that Jesus had left behind. Before Barnabas and Saul left them, by "divine providence," the disciples became known as Christians for the first time.

Sometime after this, Saul and Barnabas set out on their first missionary tour, and it was likely about this time that Saul decided to be known by his Roman name—Paul.

The ministry and missionary tours of the apostles were pretty action-packed, but none more than those of Paul. Shipwrecks, mobs, riots, beatings, stoning, imprisonment, and more plagued his ministry, but that hardly stopped the brave and highly zealous evangelizer.

Paul and Barnabas traveled through numerous cities and countries that roughly encompassed the area from modern-day Italy to Turkey and as far south as Syria and Judea. Despite their initial success in Antioch, things were not all smooth sailing for the evangelizers. They dealt with mixed reactions to their message, ranging from faith to murderous hatred.

Many times, they were forced to make a getaway for their own safety. One of the cities Paul and Barnabas fled to was Lystra, another Roman colony with many buildings and structures carved into the volcanic tuff rock the city was built upon. Their visit started with a miracle but quickly descended into chaos. Paul healed a man who had been crippled his whole life. When the man jumped up and started walking, the people believed it to be the work of their deities. They were convinced that Paul and Barnabas were gods who took the form of men, calling them Hermes and Zeus.

Wanting to show gratitude, the people insisted on sacrificing bulls to Paul and Barnabas despite the apostles' protests. It took some doing, but

---

[34] A prominent first-century Christian whose first name was Joseph. The apostles gave him the surname Barnabas, which meant "son of comfort." Like Paul, he was later styled as an apostle even though he was not one of the original twelve.

the evangelizers eventually stopped what would have been an inappropriate sacrifice to them. But the trouble in Lystra was just beginning.

Sometime later, Jews from Antioch and Iconium came down to Lystra to stir up the city against Paul and Barnabas. It worked. The crowds dragged Paul out of the city and stoned him, leaving only after they believed he was dead.[35] However, when other disciples found out and went to see whether Paul was still alive, they found he had survived. He got up and went with them back into the city. The next day, Paul and Barnabas left for Derbe. Despite the persecution, their ministry succeeded—they had made "quite a few disciples" (Acts 14:21) in the cities they visited.

Boldly, they returned to Antioch, Lystra, and Iconium to check on the new disciples and appoint elders (mature, stable men who could oversee each group) in the congregations they helped establish.

Paul, Silas, and Timothy also got mixed reviews when they reached Thessalonica, a sophisticated center of culture and trade along the *Via Egnatia*. After they spent three Sabbaths in the city synagogue reasoning with the people using scriptures, many Jews became believers. As word got around the city, many Greeks (used here by Luke to include all non-Jews) became believers, as well as quite a few prominent women of Thessalonica.

But then, as in other cities, some of the Jews became outraged by Paul and his companions. Intent on making trouble, they gathered criminals from the streets and started a riot in the city, marching over to the house where Paul and Silas were staying as guests. The crowd shouted that Paul, Silas, and other Christians were "stirring up trouble" throughout the whole world. Essentially accusing the men of sedition, the crowd claimed they opposed Caesar and supported this Jesus as king—a very dangerous claim that made the city rulers sit up and take notice. Paul and Silas were again forced to flee the city. From there, they went to Beroea (Berea), a city that may have had a very sizeable Jewish population.

Though the Beroeans (Bereans) eagerly listened to what Paul had to teach, they did not just take his word for it. Instead, they checked what

---

[35] Stoning was an ancient punishment in which large stones were thrown at an offender until they died.

he was saying against the scriptures to make sure what he was saying was true. For this, Luke called them "noble-minded." Through teaching and research, many in the city became believers, including many notable men and women of the city. But soon, Paul's Thessalonican troubles followed him to Beroea.

The Jews who had stirred up the people of Thessalonica followed Paul to Beroea to continue to stir up the people against Paul and the others. Things deteriorated again, and Paul, Silas, and Timothy were forced to leave Beroea. Paul was secreted away to Athens, and he waited for Timothy and Silas to join him there.

Paul, not one to stay idle, went about preaching while he waited for the others to reach Athens. His interactions there were quite different from those in other cities. Athens was an epicenter of religion, philosophy, and enlightened learning. Paul took the time to observe what was happening around the city and tailored his speech to the people.

However, the Epicurean and Stoic philosophers who heard him labeled Paul an ignorant "chatterer" who spouted nonsense.[36][37] Others were bewildered that he talked about a god unknown to them.[38] However, because the city was generally tolerant of new thinking and ideas, people were curious about what Paul had to say. They took him to the Areopagus, a hill that served as the site of the Athenian court system. There, he gave a clever and thought-provoking speech starting with the typical Greek opening line "Men of Athens." Although he knew what he would tell them was vastly at odds with their beliefs, he took the time to commend them for being spiritually minded.

Even though Paul carefully tailored his speech to his Greek audience, not everyone present was won over by his words. When he introduced certain teachings to the people, such as the resurrection, some scoffed in derision while others believed. Yet, many did believe. Among them were prominent Athenians, including a judge on the Areopagus council. The

---

[36] Epicureans, followers of the philosopher Epicurious, believed that pleasures and fine things were life's ultimate goal, but with moderation to avoid bad consequences.

[37] Followers of Stoic philosophies held radical ethical views and believed that a person could get rid of negative emotions like fear and envy through moral and intellectual perfectionism.

[38] Though the Roman Empire was tolerant of the wide variety of religions found within it, it was against Greek and Roman law to introduce new gods, especially if they were not in line with the existing religion of a city or region.

speech was so noteworthy and compelling that a plaque commemorating it remains at the Areopagus to this day.

Next, Paul traveled to Corinth, a relatively large, wealthy port city and center of trade with a notorious reputation for moral decadence. Here, Silas and Timothy finally met up with him. Though they again experienced some stiff and abusive opposition from a Jewish contingent, many in the city became believers. Despite this, Paul stayed for a year and a half, long enough to help establish a congregation—the same congregation to which Paul would later write two letters.

Their preaching seemed to succeed quickly in Philippi, a city along the *Via Egnatia* that had been settled by many Roman military veterans and whose people were proud of their Roman citizenship.[39]

Not all experiences involved large crowds. Some individuals and their families responded directly to the message from the apostles. One of these was in Philippi. There, they met a woman named Lydia, who was seemingly unmarried or widowed. A merchant from Thyatira, she sold clothing made from the famed purple dye of her hometown. Lydia responded favorably to the message and showed extraordinary hospitality to the preachers. Soon, she and her entire household were baptized.

One unexpected response came after a rather surprising incident.

Paul and Silas had been arrested. Deep in the lower parts of a damp prison, the men were painfully held fast in stocks. But during the night, an earthquake shook the jail, opening the cell doors and freeing all the prisoners, including Paul and Silas, from their bonds. The jailer came and saw the cell doors open and immediately assumed all the prisoners had escaped. Despondent, he was about to kill himself with his sword when Paul called out for him to stop, letting him know none had fled.[40]

The jailer, relieved and grateful, now gladly accepted Paul's message, and he and his entire family were baptized "without delay."

Though Paul and his companions were often troubled by groups of people, certain individuals caused some intense trouble. One of these

---

[39] It is possible there was no synagogue there, and some scholars believe it may be because of the strong military character of the city that Jews were not allowed to gather for worship.

[40] Ancient jailers bore a lot of responsibility for their prisoners. If any escaped, the sentence of the escapee would be imposed on the jailer. So, thinking a whole prison of inmates had escaped, the jailer naturally feared the heavy, unpleasant penalties that would be imposed on him.

was a sorcerer who went head-to-head with Paul and Barnabas.

The men had set out on their first mission to Cyprus, an island under the rule of the Roman Senate and Barnabas' native country. While there, they preached to a Roman proconsul named Sergius Paulus, who was interested in what they had to say. But the proconsul's companion, Bar-Jesus (also known as Elymas which means "sorcerer) tried to disrupt them and dissuade Sergius Paulus from believing the men. Paul did not put up with it for long. Mincing no words, he told Bar-Jesus that he was "full of every sort of fraud and every sort of villainy" before calling him a "son of the Devil" and an "enemy of everything righteous." With that, he miraculously rendered the sorcerer temporarily blind, letting him know it was from the hand of God. For his part, the proconsul was astounded by what he saw and the things Paul taught and became a believer.

Another incident in which Paul cured a demon-possessed girl soon landed him in trouble. Paul and Silas were dragged to the city magistrates by an angry mob, had their clothes torn off, and were flogged before being thrown in jail.

Sometimes, Paul and the other apostles had to overcome problems from within their ranks. After spending some time in Antioch and Jerusalem, Paul and Barnabas were ready for their second missionary tour in late 49 or early 50 AD. This mission was to check on and encourage disciples in the congregations that had formed. However, they experienced a rough start: an argument over whom they should take with them on the mission. Barnabas wanted to take John Mark.[41] In fact, Barnabas was "determined" that he come with them. Paul, however, objected on the basis that John Mark had (for some undisclosed reason) left in middle of their first mission.

"A sharp burst of anger" ensued over the matter, and the two men parted ways. Barnabas took John Mark and went on a mission to Cyprus, while Paul took Silas to visit the congregations in Syria and Cilicia.[42] This mission would take Paul back to Lystra and Derbe.

---

[41] Acts says "John, the one surnamed Mark"–the Gospel writer and a cousin of Barnabas.

[42] Silas was member of the Christian congregation in Jerusalem, likely also called by his Roman name Silvanus. Possibly the same Silvanus who later acted as Peter's secretary, helping him write the books of the Bible named after him. Silas and Timothy also helped Paul write both letters to the Thessalonians.

While in that area, Paul met a young man named Timothy. Paul was told many good things about Timothy and wanted him to accompany them. Timothy would become a good, loyal friend and lifelong traveling companion to Paul and would play an important part in the ministry and strengthening of the congregations.

Paul, Silas, and Timothy set off for Asia, but the account in Acts says that, along the way, they were blocked "by the spirit of Jesus" and redirected. So, instead, they traveled through Galatia (modern-day southern Poland and western Ukraine). Attempting to travel through Bithynia (northwestern Turkey), they were again blocked and redirected. This time, they traveled to the city of Troas in the district of Mysia (another northwest district of ancient Turkey). Once there, Paul had a divinely inspired vision in which he was instructed to preach in Macedonia (an area that today encompasses Greece, southwestern Bulgaria, and the Republic of North Macedonia).

Despite his busy preaching schedule, Paul kept in touch with what was happening in congregations he had previously established or visited. When things got tough for some, he wrote to encourage and comfort them.

While in Corinth on his second missionary tour, he wrote to the congregation in Thessalonica. Even after Paul fled from the mob violence the Jews had incited, the Christians that remained in the city continued to suffer persecution, loss, and other heavy pressures. Paul's concern moved him to write his first letter to encourage, support, and give some gentle reminders about how Christians should act.

But, sometimes, the congregations got off course, and he needed to write stronger letters of counsel to help them correct matters. Sometime after his first letter, Paul heard that some in Thessalonica were teaching inaccurate things about Jesus and had strayed from the original truths they were taught. He attempted to correct them in his second letter. He also saw that some had not followed his reminders in the first letter, so he again admonished them to behave decently as a follower of Jesus should.

Although Paul and his companions focused heavily on their ministry, they also traveled to encourage and support those who had already become Christians in various cities. That is how Paul kicked off his third missionary tour: traveling around Galatia and Phrygia to strengthen those who were already disciples. Meanwhile, Apollos was sent back to

Corinth.

Sometimes, that support came in the form of corrective teaching. A prime example of this was in Ephesus. Accompanied by Timothy and Erastus, Paul spoke in the synagogue for three months. Even though Paul used reasoning and persuasive speeches, not all accepted what he was teaching. In fact, some got up and railed against the beliefs of the Christian way.[43]

Other times, as with Thessalonica, Paul's support came in the form of letters to congregations experiencing issues. For instance, during this third missionary tour, Paul was disturbed by the reports he was getting about the congregation in Corinth. He corrected them regarding unity, immorality, and rejecting false teachings. He had also apparently received questions from the congregation, which he took the time to reply to. He wrote them two letters, now known as the Bible books of First and Second Corinthians.

Paul spent the next two years preaching in this area of Asia, but much of the action happened in Ephesus. There, Paul, accompanied by Timothy and Erastus, performed many miracles, including casting demons out of those possessed. In one incident, a demon-possessed man heartily beat up seven sons of a priest. That event put a solid fear of the wicked spirits into the people Paul was preaching to. After that, many took their books on magical arts and burned them in a huge fire, even though they were worth a lot of money. The book of Acts says after this, the Word of God spread even more, and people changed their lives according to what they had learned.

That was not the end of the action in Ephesus. A great riot was stirred up, instigated by an angry silversmith. Ephesus was famed for its grand temple to the goddess Artemis (one of the seven wonders of the ancient world). Because of this, there were many silversmiths in the city—a whole guild of them—who made and sold shrines and other religious items connected to the worship of Artemis. Paul, Gaius, Aristarchus, and other Christians began teaching that the gods the city worshipped did not exist and were no more than manmade idols. Many people in Ephesus became Christians due to this, but this denouncement did not go over well with everyone. These teachings were bad for business as far as the

---

[43] The first-century Christians called their newfound beliefs "The Way." For them, it was not just a new religion but a newly adopted way of thinking and life.

silversmiths were concerned. Demetrius, a silversmith, also worried that aside from business, the Christian teachings would also dim the magnificence of their city, temple, and gods.

Demetrius gave an angry speech, whipping the city into a frenzy. As a result, a riot ensued, and the confused mob rushed into the city's theater arena, taking Gaius and Aristarchus with them. Paul tried to follow but was stopped by fellow Christians and some concerned city officials.

Inside the arena, the people loudly yelled about various things, most not even knowing why they were there. Finally, a Jewish man named Alexander was pushed forward to calm the crowds. Alexander had a real challenge on his hands. On seeing that he was a Jew, the crowds chanted, "Great is Artemis of the Ephesians!" for two hours, not letting him get a word out.

A city official finally stepped in to help. He declared that Paul and the others had broken no laws, but the crowd was in imminent danger of being charged with sedition. He told them that if they had a problem, it should go through the proper legal channels—not an angry mob scene. His words hit their mark, and the crowd dispersed.

After this, Paul, Timothy, Aristarchus, Sopater, and several others decided to travel back to Macedonia through Greece, stopping at several places. After a few months and a side trip to Syria to avoid a plot by the Jews, Paul knew his ministry was coming to an end. He told the others that the Holy Spirit was leading him towards Jerusalem, where he would face imprisonment. Along the way, he said tearful goodbyes to many in the congregations he had helped form and strengthen. He did not go alone. At least Luke accompanied him to Jerusalem, where he *was* arrested and began a different phase of his life and ministry.

The rest of the apostles and missionaries continued their work in preaching and with the congregations. But the Christians had reached a new phase. Their foundations were being solidified, and Christians were spreading the word wherever they were.

Chapter 4: The First Church

Though the apostles and other Christians preached with wildly varying results, until 36 AD, their focus was on persuading the Jewish population that Jesus was the Messiah and had instituted a new way.[44] The Jews were the first priority, so the apostles started in the city with perhaps the greatest concentration of Jewish people—Jerusalem. It's no surprise, then, that this is where the first Christian congregation was also established. But who was going to lead it?

There is no indication in the scriptures that one particular man was the congregation's leader, but the apostles John, James, and Peter were mentioned as pillars, with the dynamic Peter characteristically taking the lead as spokesman on many occasions.[45] They were not alone to shoulder the responsibility of the growing Christian discipleship. Others besides the twelve apostles, referred to as "older men" or elders, helped oversee the congregation in Jerusalem.

However, there were many Jewish people and communities outside of Jerusalem and Judea. The Diaspora, or dispersed Jews, had settled far and wide, hence the need for a preaching campaign. Though the Judeo-Christians were preaching to people of the same background, it is evident from Acts that they did not always receive a warm welcome.

---

[44] After that, the message was opened up to Gentiles, or non-Jewish people.
[45] This was the apostle James. After his death, Jesus' half-brother James replaced him in the governing body.

Though they had long awaited the Messiah, not all Jews accepted the teachings of Jesus, and many were even hostile towards them. As we saw from the previous account of Paul's travels, the Christians had some success in speaking to the common Jewish people, yet some were vehemently opposed to the spread of these new teachings. The Jewish religious leaders had the apostles arrested and brought before the Jewish high court on several occasions and the apostles were imprisoned multiple times for their message.[46]

Yet, there was a lot of positive response as well, particularly from the Greek-speaking Jewish communities.

Many Jews had migrated and settled throughout the Mediterranean region, living in cities surrounded by Hellenistic culture and Greek-speaking neighbors. It was inevitable that Greek culture and ideas would seep into Jewish communities. Still, these migrants continued to practice their Jewish religion and traveled to Jerusalem for the annual Jewish festivals.

Greek Influences

Even though the Roman Empire reigned supreme at the time, Greek culture was still a hot trend (even for the Romans). The early Christians weren't totally immune to its influence and, in some ways, adapted their message to a Greek-obsessed Mediterranean world.

The apostle Paul had a real knack for this. Highly educated, he was familiar with many Greek philosophical concepts, such as those of the Stoics and Epicureans. Paul found common ground even among people with completely opposite outlooks. He cited poets like Aratus and Cleanthes to support his points and used understood concepts and terms to explain his message.

Paul also referenced Greek life in his teachings, using well-known cultural icons like the "temple of the unknown god" and athletic games such as foot races to help make his points come to life in a way people would understand. Some Greek words, such as *karpos*, meaning fruit or fruitage, were used metaphorically by the Christians to explain concepts or paint a picture that could be easily understood and embraced.

It wasn't just Greek life that colored the writings of the first-century Christians. Many books now in the Bible were either written or

---

[46] Though, on more than one occasion, they were miraculously freed from prison.

translated into Greek to reach a wider audience.[47] They borrowed Greek terms, Greek sentence structures and style, and ancient Greek pop culture. But one thing the first-century Christians adamantly rejected was philosophical or pagan Greek religious beliefs. Many Greek teachings clashed hard with Christian values, so Christians were admonished not to mix Greek-inspired beliefs with what they were taught. In fact, in several letters Paul wrote to the congregations, he highlighted the need to avoid the influence of these sorts of Greek teachings—quite a feat in a world dominated by them.

On the other hand, Judaism had mixed itself with Greek culture and thinking to some extent, thanks in part to prominent Jews like the first-century writer Philo. Philo was a fan of certain concepts taught by the Greek philosopher Plato, although he was not entirely sold on what the famed thinker had to say. Still, Plato influenced him to accept the teaching on the immortality of the soul—something not taught or accepted by the apostles and most first-century Christians, nor most Jews for that matter. Philo was not a Christian or a convert, but his ideas influenced some professed Christians, including other Christian writers who accepted his concept. In part, this concept may have found its way into the thinking of some Christians through Jewish converts to Christianity.

The immortality of the soul was not the only Greek concept to make its way into some Jewish and Christian circles. Philo's take on the Greek word *logos* (meaning reason, or the word), along with the influences of Plato, Aristotle, and the Stoics, also formed the basis for a teaching that became popular in Christendom later on—the Trinity.[48]

The shadows of Hellenization could also be discerned in the works of later writers such as Clement, Origen, and Eusebius. Subsequent generations of Christian writers, including Gregory of Nazianzus

---

[47] As the Greek language dominated society, Hebrew was pushed into the background, even among Jews. The meaning and understanding of important scriptures written in Hebrew would be lost to vast swaths of the population unless it could be translated into Greek. Through the last three centuries BCE, Jewish scholars meticulously translated Hebrew scripture into Greek. The result? What is today known as the Greek Septuagint version of the Hebrew scriptures. The translation into Greek was an epic game-changer. Without this translation into Greek, the context of the Christian message could not have been understood on such a large scale. People of diverse backgrounds and cultures could now understand the important history and concepts that led to Christianity.

[48] The word "trinity" is not found in the Bible writings.

(dubbed the "Christian Demosthenes") and Gregory of Nyssa (who also had a trendy moniker—"the Father of Mysticism") turned out poetry and other artistic works that were said to rival those of the Greeks.[49]

Though Greek teachings, religion, and philosophy were all but nonexistent in the original Christian congregations, the language and culture influenced first-century Christian writings. However, Greek philosophy slowly began to permeate the works and teachings of later Christian writers, as will be seen later on.

---

[49] Demosthenes was a Greek statesman, orator, and prolific speech writer.

Chapter 5: Early Christian Communities

As the number of Christians grew, so did the need for responsible men to get things organized and operating. Some of these responsible men, mature Christians, joined the apostles to comprise a central "governing body" that oversaw the expansion of the Christian congregations. They also gave instructions, clarified doctrinal teachings, and made decisions based on scriptures and Jesus' teachings. This governing body helped appoint elders in other congregations and appointed overseers to help with special projects like relief collection and food distribution to Christians in famine-plagued areas.[50] The elders also had assistants who helped them with non-spiritual tasks within the congregation. These men were called *diakonos*, a broad term for minister (some translate it as deacon).

For the most part, early Christians were on board with this structure, though some had to be counseled for being too prominence-oriented. Yet, there was no real "ladder" to climb. Being given oversight meant more responsibility, which most shouldered admirably. None were paid; it was voluntary self-sacrifice to work for the good of the congregation, done out of love and passion for the work. Leaders were regular men with secular jobs and families to care for. Christians saw this way of doing things as God's arrangement guided by the Holy Spirit.

---

[50] Men who were responsible for the care of the congregation.

One of the greatest tasks of the governing body was organizing the preaching work. This was a massive undertaking. Jesus' apostles and disciples were initially tasked with preaching to Jewish people "of all nations." This would be difficult for their small numbers. Jews were spread throughout the Roman Empire and spoke many different languages. However, the current disciples only spoke a few of these. How could they possibly get this job done?

Acts 2:1-4 tells of a miracle among a gathered group of disciples that made this widespread preaching possible: "Suddenly there was a noise from heaven, just like that of a rushing, stiff breeze, and it filled the whole house where they were sitting. And tongues as if of fire became visible to them and were distributed, and one came to rest on each one of them, and they all became filled with holy spirit and started to speak in different languages, just as the spirit enabled them to speak."

Given the miraculous ability to speak in foreign languages, the disciples could now preach to Jews from other nations. Jews from all over the Roman Empire and beyond were gathered in Jerusalem for a religious festival at the time, and the disciples preached to them in their native languages.

The people were stunned, but the reception was mixed. Some were "perplexed" as to how it was possible they were being spoken to in their own language, and others thought that the disciples were drunk. Peter, however, quickly cleared things up. In a speech to the crowd, he told them that the disciples were not drunk at all; the Holy Spirit had given them this miraculous ability. From then on, word about Jesus and all he had done spread ever faster.

But it wasn't until 36 CE that the job of preaching broadened considerably. It all started with a Gentile (non-Jewish person) named Cornelius. A wealthy man of status, Cornelius was a Roman centurion (a military commander in charge of 100 soldiers) in the city of Caesarea. Despite his elite status, Cornelius often used his wealth to help the needy. Although he wasn't a Jew or a convert, Acts describes him and his family as devout and God-fearing.

One afternoon, Cornelius was praying when an angel approached him in a vision. The angel told him that God had seen his good works and sincerely devout nature and taken special note of it. He was directed to summon the apostle Peter, who was in another city thirty miles away. The next day, Peter got the memo in the form of his own perplexing vision. Just as he walked downstairs, trying to figure out what the vision could possibly mean, the men from Cornelius came knocking at his door. Peter went with him, and long story short, Cornelius and his entire household were baptized. They became some of the first non-Jewish Christian proselytes, and under divine guidance given to Peter, the door to Christianity was now open to everyone, no matter their religion or background. With that, Christianity took off on a whole new level.

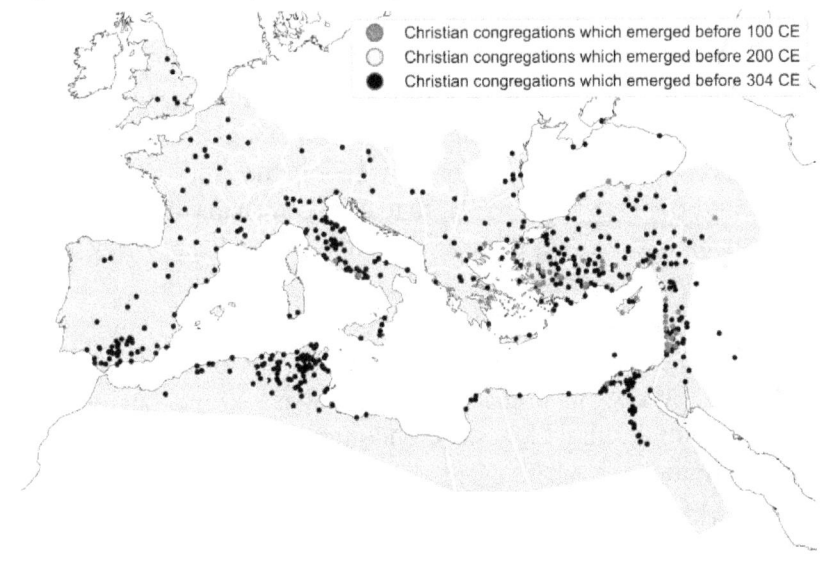

Distribution of Christian congregations in the first three centuries.
Jan Fousek, Vojtěch Kaše, Adam Mertel, Eva Výtvarová, Aleš Chalupa. Citation: Fousek J, Kaše V, Mertel A, Výtvarová E, Chalupa A (2018) Spatial constraints on the diffusion of religious innovations: The case of early Christianity in the Roman Empire. PLoS ONE 13(12): e0208744. https://doi.org/10.1371/journal.pone.0208744, CC BY-SA 4.0
<https://creativecommons.org/licenses/by-sa/4.0>, via Wikimedia Commons; https://commons.wikimedia.org/wiki/File:Distribution_of_the_documented_presence_of_Christian_congregations_in_the_first_three_centuries.tif

For Jewish and Gentile converts alike, Christianity was not simply about changing their religion; it was an entirely new way of life—a whole different culture. The foundation of that culture was love. Not romantic love (Greek *eros*) but love based on principle and true family-like affection (Greek *agape* and *philia*). That *philia*—brotherly love—inspired Christians to call one another brother and sister.

That love was to be without prejudice—race, background, class, social status, and occupation didn't matter. That's not to say that some Christians didn't have their hurdles to overcome regarding ingrained prejudices—even the apostle Peter struggled for a while. But Paul preached that God welcomed all who wanted to learn about him without bias and that those in the congregations should do the same. So, the early congregations had a wide range of ethnic and social diversity—from free men to slaves, from the uneducated to the highly educated, from lower class to nobles. They were tentmakers, fishermen, soldiers, weavers, merchants, nobles, prominent citizens, officials in the emperor's court, senators, and people from all backgrounds. Yet, they were not split apart by their differences. Love bound them together.

Jesus said this type of love would identify them as his true disciples, and it became a hallmark of their culture. It affected everything they did and said, even when life and death were on the line. Second-century Christian author Tertullian wrote that non-Christians noticed this love that Christians had among themselves and observed that "they are even ready to die for one another."

Christians didn't limit their love to just one another. They worked at being good neighbors to everyone. Their love was about more than just not harming others or doing immoral things. It was an active and proactive type of caring. They were encouraged to be forces for good in their communities.

They worked and lived modestly to provide for themselves and their families and have a little extra in case others were in need. Arrangements were made to care for widows, orphans, and others who needed help within the congregation. In some cases, those who had the means sold property and possessions and pooled their resources, giving what they had to the apostles arranging the distribution. This arrangement was very effective—so much so that Acts 4:34 says that "there was no one among them in need."

Christians didn't just help those in their immediate area but were part of an interconnected network that stretched as far as there were congregations. The first recorded example of Christian relief work took place during the reign of Roman Emperor Claudius. There was a famine in Judea, and most of the poor had no resources to acquire food. Christians in Antioch took stock of what they could give and, with the help of Paul and Barnabas, arranged for relief contributions to be sent to Judea.

Interestingly, all the funds collected were given voluntarily and distributed by volunteers. No one gave because they were embarrassed or forced into it, took a cut of the money, or were paid for their efforts in distributing (some of which took considerable time, effort, and travel). It was all done out of love and care for each other. Everything that was collected went directly toward caring for those who needed it.

Not long after that, near the beginning of Roman Emperor Nero's reign in 55 CE, many Christians in Judea were still struggling with poverty. Paul headed up a massive collection effort by the congregations in Galatia, Achaia, and Macedonia. In 56 CE, they took everything they collected. Paul, accompanied by several Christian men for safety's sake, personally delivered the contributions to those in Judea.

Aside from helping one another, Christians were law-abiding citizens. They viewed the governmental authorities—yes, even the much-hated Romans—as allowed by God to be in their positions. Law and order brought a measure of peace and stability to their society, and they did their part to cooperate, as it benefited all. They did not want to take those benefits without giving back.

Christians quietly paid their taxes, even though for many of the Jews, the taxes were a real sore point and the catalyst for violent clashes over the years. They also willingly performed whatever civic duties the government asked of them, applying the principle Jesus spoke of in Matthew 5:41: "If someone under authority impresses you into service for a mile, go with him two miles."

There were, however, limits to their compliance. Although Christians obeyed governmental authorities, they obeyed God first and foremost. So, if they were commanded or compelled to do something that went against God's laws and principles or their trained consciences, that is where their compliance with human laws ended. For example, there were many instances when the apostles and disciples were imprisoned and commanded to stop preaching. Their response? "We must obey God as ruler rather than men." They would not allow anything the authorities commanded to jeopardize their relationship with God.

The lives of first-century Christians revolved around spiritual matters. There are many examples in the Bible and the testimony of writers like Tertullian, who spoke about the Christians meeting together to discuss, teach, and listen to the holy writings. When some of the Hebrew-speaking Christians slacked off in this area, Paul reminded them not to "forsake the gathering of themselves together." This was for their benefit and to encourage others they met with. This made the congregational arrangement beneficial to all who participated.

They also made preaching and Christian teaching a focus in their lives. Both men and women went from house to house in an organized fashion, the most efficient way to ensure everyone heard the message. They also tried to reach those in the markets and other public places.

Despite the good works and love among the Christians, they were still imperfect people. They experienced real problems like anyone else. Paul and the other apostles had to give counsel on numerous occasions, warning that some congregations needed to get their act together. The Christians were to maintain high moral conduct, but not everyone did so. Some were mixed up in dishonest behavior and immorality; others became apostates promoting sects, drunkards, extortioners, and slanders. In one case, a man was sleeping with his father's wife. Many turned around when corrected, but a few were unrepentant, and these weren't allowed to stick around and influence others. They were removed from the congregation so as not to contaminate its moral cleanness.

Flaws and all, the early Christians strived to maintain the right balance between being good family members, citizens, congregation members, and, most of all, good in God's eyes. But they were still refining themselves to get it right according to what Jesus taught.

Chapter 6: Removal of Jewish Characteristics

While it's true that Jesus and some of the apostles laid down some scathing words on the Jewish Pharisees, his purpose was not to create animosity between his followers and the Jews. However, many of the Jewish religious leaders were offended by the continued proselytizing and conversion of Jews to Christianity. Aside from that, one of the biggest points of contention between Jews and Christians was the identity of the long-awaited Messiah.

Even though there was continuity between Jewish beliefs and the teachings of Christians, the gap between them was obvious. Both groups believed in one Almighty God, believed the Hebrew Scriptures were sacred and divinely inspired, highly regarded the prophets and faithful men of ancient times, and rejected pagan beliefs. The Gospels can't be read without bumping into copious quotes and citations from the Hebrew Scriptures. These Jewish teachings and beliefs comprised a body of information that pointed to the Messiah. But just who that was and what his purpose was—well, that is where their paths diverged.

Christians taught that the old Jewish belief system was replaced by the new way that Jesus had started. His death had started a new covenant in which the Jewish people were no longer solely God's chosen people, but God's acceptance of their worship was contingent on their acceptance of Jesus as the Messiah. "Out with the old and in with the new" did not sit well with everyone. This proved to be true even among Jews-turned-Christians.

Perhaps one of the most hotly debated topics of the day was circumcision. Jewish law required all males to be circumcised eight days after being born. And if a man were a convert to Judaism, the requirement of circumcision still stood, even though it would be far more memorable as an adult. Many Jewish Christians felt that the requirement also applied to Gentile men who converted to Christianity. They argued that they would need to be circumcised to be approved by God.

Paul and Barnabas strongly argued with those in the congregations in Syria, Antioch, and Cilicia against the Christian need for circumcision. Since they couldn't agree on such a sensitive topic, the matter was brought to the central governing body in Jerusalem to sort out.

Peter was the first to speak in favor of not adding the burden of circumcision to Christians. James, speaking next, backed him up. The decision from the whole governing body was a unanimous vote to not impose circumcision on *anyone*—probably to the great relief of many. This decision was just one area in which the Christians were leaving their former Jewish customs behind.

Under Jewish law, certain animals (such as pigs) were considered unclean to eat and were never found on the dinner table of a law-abiding Jewish person. But one day, Peter had a vision, and pork, among other formerly forbidden foods, was now allowed on the menu. In this vision, recorded in Acts 10:11-15, Peter saw a large sheet come down from heaven, and all sorts of four-footed animals, birds, and reptiles were on it. A voice from heaven told Peter to eat. Peter was horrified—he would never dare eat an unclean animal. Three times, the voice assured him it was okay to eat, giving divine permission to have whatever meat they saw fit. However, it is nearly certain that many Jewish Christians had the same repulsed reaction as Peter. Later, Paul told the Corinthians that if they were guests in someone's house, to "eat whatever is put before you."[51]

---

[51] Here, Paul was primarily talking about meats offered to pagan gods and then sold in the market. Some Christians objected to eating these because they had been used in pagan rites. However, he would not have told the congregation to eat whatever they were served if there were divine restrictions on certain meats.

Another avenue where Christianity diverged from Jewish custom was in the socializing between Jews and Gentiles. The two groups previously did not mix socially, let alone eat together. According to Jewish religious leaders, any Jew who even *entered* the house of a non-Jew was considered ceremonially unclean. Peter, after converting Cornelius to Christianity, set a precedent for eating meals with Gentile Christians and apparently did so for the next thirteen years—that was until he landed in Syrian Antioch. Many Jewish Christians had been slow to shed their previous ways of thinking and doing, and this was one thing they strictly adhered to.

When Peter found out some Jewish Christians were coming in from Jerusalem, he suddenly abandoned mealtime with Gentile Christians, pretending it never happened out of fear of being ostracized by the visitors. The other Jewish Christians followed suit, with even Barnabas jumping in on the charade. Paul, however, caught wind of what was happening and gently but firmly corrected them. All Christians should be unified regardless of background.

What Peter and the others had done was not just a matter of meal habits. By adopting that attitude, they would be all but voiding the decision made by the governing body in Jerusalem. When they made their decision on circumcision, the governing body had concluded their words by saying, "For the holy spirit_and we ourselves have favored adding no further burden to you except these necessary things: to keep abstaining from things sacrificed to idols, from blood, from what is strangled, and from sexual immorality." Effectively, they declared the Mosaic Law no longer binding for Christians—everyone only needed to follow the new way.

In general, the Christians were not slowly separating themselves from their Jewish roots in a bid to cause division. Their whole goal was to help the Jewish people understand Jesus' teachings. And, for the most part, they tried to do it with love.

A good example is a well-known second-century dialogue between Justin Martyr, a Christian, and the Jewish Trypho. Rather than being confrontational, Justin appealed to his Jewish companion by first assuring him that he had the utmost respect for the Jewish people. Justin used persuasive words tempered with a brotherly tone to convince Trypho that Jesus is the Messiah. Though in the end they agreed to disagree, they parted as friends.

Certainly not all interactions between Jews and Christians went that well, but it helps show the complex and varied dynamic between the groups. However, it wasn't long before it was just the Jewish beliefs that Christians departed from - many began to depart from the original teachings of Christianity itself.

Chapter 7: One Religion, Many Versions

The apostles John and Paul called it correctly (under divine inspiration). By the end of the first century, deviation from the original teachings of Jesus and the apostles had begun. The mixing of philosophies and other religious ideas, old and new, gave birth to many new offshoots that operated under the banner of Christianity.

One of these movements, Gnosticism, got a foothold in the first century but had started to become popular by the second century AD. Partly mystical, partly Stoic philosophy, among other things, Gnosticism is believed by some scholars to have been started by a magician named Simon, who is referenced in the book of Acts.[52]

The idea of being aware of deeply hidden mystical things, such as the special knowledge embedded in Bible numbers, appealed to some. The concepts behind Gnosticism were nothing new, even for the first century. Gnostics took little bits from here and there—a dash of Judaism, a smattering of ideas from ancient cultures like Babylon and Egypt, a few concepts from eastern religions, and later, a sprinkling of Christianity.[53]

---

[52] Unlike the sleight-of-hand magicians of today, Simon practiced magical arts connected to the occult.

[53] Some of the eastern religious concepts included were things like balances of good and evil—yin and yang

According to Gnosticism, the God of the Jews and Christians was not the almighty Creator but a lesser god who ruled one of 345 heavens. They believed that the creation of the universe was a big, reckless mistake by a more supreme deity named Sophia (or Wisdom). With the help of a semi-divine "craftsman", Sophia inadvertently created a world (earth) that was simply a copy of another existing realm. The malevolent craftsman, Demiurge (corresponding the Christian and Jewish Almighty God Yahweh) had an obvious bias for the Jewish people and set himself up in this world as the only existing god, angering other, higher deities. If that wasn't enough to cause the first church fathers to declare Gnosticism a heresy, there was more. Demiurge, an angry, jealous sort, causes all kinds of problems on earth because of his favoritism. In a bid to save humans from all this trouble, the gods of the other 364 heavens sent Jesus Christ to Earth as a rescuer. A later Gnostic philosopher, Basilides, declared that Jesus did not actually die. His death was a delusion or vision.

Though these beliefs were deemed heresy, not everyone agreed. Some, like the Gnostic teacher Valentinus, believed the movement meshed well with Christian teachings. Instead of contradicting Christian teachings, some Gnostic teachers put a spin on the original teachings, infusing them with a Stoic flavor at times. They traded the ideas of sin and repentance for the concepts of sin and faith as consequences of merely existing. Instead of salvation being open to anyone, it was only available to those with special mystical knowledge. Instead of freedom through Jesus' sacrifice, it was attained by denying oneself any bodily desires.

Inconsistent and difficult to comprehend, Gnosticism was largely rejected by early Christians as an aberration encased in a thinly veiled layer of Christianity.

Possibly cropping up as the Temple of Jerusalem was destroyed by the Romans in 70 AD, the Ebionites sprang from a splinter group of Jewish Christians. With no archaeological evidence to support their existence, they might have forever stayed in obscurity if it weren't for the accounts of their critics. Justin Martyr and Irenaeus mention them, but the most complete account was written by Epiphanius in the fourth century, even though what he says about them only provides a general description. The Ebionites were among eighty sects that Epiphanius denounced as heretical.

The heretic label was fastened to the Ebionites due to their mixing of Judaism and Christianity. Though it may seem similar, the Ebionites should not be mistaken for Jewish Christians. There was a big difference. Jewish Christians were Jewish by birth and converted to Christianity, fully adopting the Christian faith and accepting that they were no longer under Jewish law. The Ebionites, however, were Jewish Christians who adopted the fundamentals of Christian teachings but "stubbornly clung" to Jewish law, holding it as an obligation, even though Christians were no longer under the Mosaic (Jewish) law.[54] They maintained that since Jesus was a Jew who used the Mosaic Law in his teachings, it was the right way to live.

Like the Jews and Christians, they believed in one Almighty God, but unlike Jews or Christians, they believed in Jesus with a certain twist. They reportedly only embraced Matthew's Gospel except for the virgin birth part.[55] They believed that Jesus was a true prophet and the awaited Messiah but did not have a divine origin. As far as they were concerned, he was a regular human and the natural son of both Mary *and* Joseph. The only reason he could claim Messiah status was that he strictly followed Jewish law—a lofty example that they strived to imitate. Sure, he was a great example, and one had to listen to his teachings to find the Kingdom of God, but many Ebionites did not believe his sacrifice covered their sins.

Still, the Ebionites didn't hold onto *all* Jewish practices. They deemed the long-standing practice of animal sacrifices no longer necessary or required due to the distinctly Christian belief that Jesus' death was a final sacrifice covering their sins. Part of their resistance to completely moving away from Jewish law might have been fueled by the opening of Christianity to the Gentiles and their "anything goes" diet. The Ebionites preferred to strictly adhere to Jewish dietary guidelines and the no-fraternizing-with-Gentiles rule of the past. The Christian congregation was now a melting pot of cultures, and they could not accept that.

It wasn't just the Gentiles the Ebionites took issue with. They also had a big problem with the Apostle Paul, who had been a Jewish Pharisee before he saw the literal light of the Lord on the road and converted.

---

[54] As per the words of Irenaeus

[55] They later also found Matthew's Gospel unsatisfactory and reworked it, naming their book the Gospel of Ebionites. There is no surviving text of this work.

Regarding him as an apostate, the Ebionites completely rejected his writings. Unlike them, Paul taught the end of Jewish law and practiced it, too—one of the things that led the Ebionites to conclude he was not as faithful to the teachings of Jesus as they were. Per Epiphanius, the hot gossip among the Ebionites was that Paul was not born a Jew but was a Greek convert who scandalously adopted Judaism solely to marry the daughter of the high priest. But the word was that she rejected him, leading to his apostasy.

Speaking of apostasy, the irony here was that, as the first few centuries wore on, the Ebionites held more faithfully to the original Christian teachings than most who professed to be fully Christian. They rejected ideas that had crept into Christian teachings, such as the Trinity, but kept the teachings about God's Kingdom and its future role, Jesus having a pre-human existence in heaven, and the governing body of Jerusalem taking the lead among early Christians as opposed to just Peter.

The Ebionites, however, were not the only Judeo-Christian sect. Closely linked to these were the Nazarenes. Some Christian writers of the first few centuries differentiated between the two groups. Some mistook them for Jews. Jerome, on the other hand, believed the Ebionites and Nazarenes were one and the same. But with no surviving information from the time, there is no concrete way to know why he believed this.

In the book of Acts, non-Christians referred to Christianity as the "sect of the Nazarenes," perhaps due to Jesus being from Nazareth. It's possible that non-Christians confused facts and used an inaccurate label or lumped all those who believed in Jesus into one group.

The Nazarenes seemed to have a lot in common with Ebionites in that they, too, held onto the Jewish customs and law. Another thing they held in common was their distaste for Paul (ironic, since he is accused of being the ringleader of the "sect of the Nazarenes" in Acts 24:5), likely due to his preaching that Jewish law was now obsolete. And this is where the Nazarenes diverged from the Ebionites. The Ebionites believed that *everyone* needed to adhere to Jewish law, while the Nazarenes believed that it was only necessary for those born Jews.

Whichever beliefs they leaned toward, the Nazarenes were not the same Nazarenes referenced in Paul's day. It seems that the later Nazarenes faded into obscurity by the fifth century, the last time they are mentioned in writing. But they weren't the last of the Judeo-Christian sects mentioned.

The enigmatic Elkesaites emerged in the early second century.[56] Who were they? It is almost hard to say as they seemed to have an identity crisis regarding what they believed. Though the Elkesaites adopted some Christian beliefs or versions of them, their doctrines held a distinct Gnostic edge. Yet they were closely associated with the highly disciplined Jewish Essene sect. They also picked and borrowed from some Eastern pagan religions, mixing naturalism, astronomy, and magic and using the stars to pick auspicious dates for important events like baptism.

Like other Judeo-Christian sects, Elkesaites were staunchly obligated to Jewish laws such as observing the Sabbath, facing Jerusalem when praying, and, in particular, the very divisive matter of circumcision. But they cast aside one of the main tenets of Jewish law: animal sacrifices. They may not have fully agreed with the other sects on certain matters, but one thing they all embraced was a rejection of Paul and his writings.

Although later more "Christianized," the Elkesaites were less committal than full-fledged Christians, their views on Jesus bordering on ambiguous. They did support the virgin birth of Jesus. However, some thought he was just an angel, while others adopted a reincarnation view of the Christ—a continuous cycle of him dying and being reborn to earth, a cycle that started with Adam. Like early Christians, they celebrated what is commonly called the Lord's Supper, originally a commemoration of Jesus.[57] death. Like early Christians, the Elkesaites were big proponents of marriage. However, they believed it was okay to leave their faith when persecution got a bit too fiery.

So, how did Gnosticism come into the mix? A great example is the Elkesaites' main holy book, writings that were not part of the Torah or the Bible. The book of Elxai (Elchasai), a strong influence among the sect, was reported by Origen to have fallen straight from heaven. (Other accounts say it was given by an angel). In true Gnostic fashion, the book's contents could only be revealed to a person who was sworn to secrecy never to reveal its words.

---

[56] Alternately spelled Elcesaites. There are varying opinions about how they got their name—a town called Elksai, a mysterious founder named Elxai, or the name of the chief holy book of the sect.

[57] Also referred to as the Last Supper and the Lord's Evening Meal.

But how did some of the early Church Fathers feel about the book? Epiphanius said the book was for people who were "neither Jews nor Christians nor pagans" but for those who stood firmly in the middle ground of these three religious ideologies. As the Catholic Encyclopedia puts it, the Elkesaite creed was a "wild medley of heathen superstitions" mixed with Christianity and Judaism, making the Elkesaites one of the hardest groups to define. They seemed to defy any one category of religion.

Although few contemporary texts discuss these groups, there is abundant evidence that, by the second century, Christian or pseudo-Christian beliefs had found their way into other religious groups or were mixed with other teachings. What the apostle John had written came true: after the apostles died, the original Christian teachings became diluted.

Chapter 8: The First Church Fathers

Who were the men who took the lead in the early Christian congregations, and what were their stories? Important to the history of Christianity and fascinating for their faith and monumental deeds, here are the stories of some of the men who left their mark on Christianity in the first few centuries.

Of course, we must start with some of the apostles, men who helped form the original governing body of Jerusalem and made some of the most important decisions in the history of Christianity.

Not much is known about Peter's personal life other than that he was a married fisherman who sometimes acted a bit rash. Nonetheless, he was known to be bold, courageous, and fiercely loyal by nature. He was one of those considered "unlettered and ordinary"[58] by the Pharisees. Yet when Jesus called Peter to be his follower, Peter dropped everything without hesitation. His life became anything but ordinary.

Outgoing with a big, colorful personality, Peter was, unsurprisingly, the spokesman for the apostles. Jesus also gave him the important metaphorical "keys of the kingdom." What did they unlock? Returning to Peter's vision of the animals coming down from heaven, we see that it was not just about getting to eat tasty meats. It had a second meaning.

---

[58] This did not mean he could not read and write; rather, he had no formal education from a rabbinical school and held no position of status within the Jewish ranks.

Previously, the Jews viewed the Gentiles as "unclean," but in the vision, Peter was told to "stop calling unclean what God has called clean."

Those keys, as they were called, opened the message to three distinct groups: the Jews and Jewish converts, the Samaritans, and the Gentiles.[59] Jesus had told Peter in John 21:15-17 that when he was no longer with them, Peter should "feed his little sheep," meaning he was to play a major role in caring for the disciples spiritually. The main way Peter did this was through preaching and organizing the preaching work done by other disciples. With Peter taking the lead, everyone would have the opportunity to hear what Jesus had preached and decide whether to be baptized into the Christian way.

Peter shouldered a huge responsibility, but how did he feel about his role among fellow Christians? Interestingly, nowhere does Peter make decisions for anyone or claim a spot as the head of the Christian congregations. Instead, he referred to himself as an "older man" or "elder" and an apostle, working with the other elders and apostles appointed. Despite his sometimes-brash beginnings, Peter's later humility was highlighted when he stopped Cornelius from kneeling, prostrating himself, or rendering any form of worship to him.

Aside from preaching and making important decisions, Peter had been given the power to perform miracles. He is mentioned as healing two men on two separate occasions and was also the first apostle to perform a resurrection when he raised a woman named Tabitha from the dead.

Not everyone was a fan of Peter. He particularly raised the ire of Judean ruler Herod Agrippa I. Wanting nothing more than to see Peter dead, he passed a death sentence down on the apostle. No doubt Jesus' words from years ago telling Peter he would die a martyr's death were ringing in his ears. However, this was not the time. Just hours before he was set to be executed, Peter escaped from his guards and out of Herod's grasp with the help of an angel.

However, death and martyrdom would still find Peter. Although the Bible does not specify how he died, in the most common version of his death, Emperor Nero catches up with him during the persecution of

---

[59] Samaritans were half-Jewish people who had adopted some Jewish customs and beliefs, such as high regard for the first five books of the Hebrew Scriptures. However, they were not considered part of the Jewish nation.

Christians in Rome.[60] The historian Eusebius wrote that Peter, bound and led away, died the same way Jesus did—hung on a stake. But according to Eusebius, there was a twist: Peter asked to be hung upside down because he felt unworthy to die in the same manner as his master. There is no evidence of which version is accurate, if any.

Undoubtedly a pillar of the early congregation, Peter wasn't the only one shouldering responsibility for the young fledgling Christian group. Many other responsible men were doing their share. One of these was Jesus' half-brother, James.

Growing up with Jesus, James did not see his brother as the Messiah. He may have even been among Jesus' relatives and townsmen who thought he had lost his mind when he started his ministry. It wasn't until after his brother's death that James changed his thinking.

A resurrected Jesus made a personal appearance to James. While the Bible doesn't describe the exchange or how James reacted, it apparently convinced James that his brother was indeed the Messiah. He became a believer and may have had a hand in convincing his other brothers, who also became believers.

In fact, James was so thoroughly convinced of Jesus' identity that he became a prominent leader in Jerusalem. Dubbed an apostle (in the broad sense of the word) James was named as one of those who "seemed to be pillars"—an indication of his great support to the early Christians and their work. James was among those making important decisions, one of the most noteworthy of which was weighing in on the circumcision debate. Besides Peter, his is the only other recorded speech on the matter.

Interestingly, the books of Galatians and Acts note that Peter and Paul reported important events to James, and he was even among the elders who gave Paul advice when rumors about him started to escalate. But it wasn't just to Paul that he gave advice. One of his greatest contributions to Christianity came in the form of a letter known by his name. In the book of James, he gives advice on the importance of drawing close to God, endurance, patience, love, faith, and self-examination. He also warns about letting fleshly desires get the better of a Christian, the bad kind of pride, going back on your word, the pitfalls of riches and corruption, keeping the tongue under control, the

---

[60] There are numerous versions of how Peter died, as many as fifteen different stories.

dubiousness of faith without actions to back it up, and favoritism.

But none of the prominence, responsibilities, or even the fact that he was the physical brother of Jesus (a fact he doesn't mention) caused him to be haughty or arrogant—absolutely the opposite. Tradition has it that he was called "James the Just," a testament to the type of person he was.

Although the Bible doesn't say how he died, Josephus fills in the story. While Judea was between governors after the death of Festus in 62 AD, the Jewish high priest Ananias and the Sanhedrin jumped on the opportunity to mete out punishment to James and other Christians. The harshest penalty for allegedly breaking Jewish law was handed down—death by stoning.

James and Peter weren't the only ones who died for their Christian faith. There were many—some who were named in history, and some who died unknown to modern Christendom. As the original apostles and those labeled apostles in the first century died, some of their contemporaries wrote works that were not included in the Bible canon. These men are often referred to as "Apostolic Fathers"—men who either knew one of the twelve apostles personally or were separated from them by one degree, having been taught by disciples who learned directly from the apostles[61]. Some consider what they wrote the most historically valuable writings outside of the Christian Greek Scriptures/New Testament.

As the ship the man was forced onto made its way to sea, the other men aboard began to fasten a rope around him. At the end of that rope was tied an anchor, an object that would forever symbolize the man tied to it. Who was he, and how did he come into this predicament? More importantly, is his story true?

Not much is historically known about the life of Clement of Rome. Tertullian and Irenaeus list him as a contemporary of the apostles, and he may have even been an eyewitness to their preaching. Some scholars wonder if he was the Clement mentioned by Paul in his letter to the Philippian congregation. However, it's unlikely, as traditionally he was not presented as a big fan of Paul.

---

[61] The Apostolic Fathers lived between the first and second centuries. Men known as "Church Fathers" lived between the second and fifth centuries.

But Clement is believed to have written his own letter, the *First Letter of Clement*, to the Corinthian Christians to help sort out a controversy over leadership there.[62] After setting them straight about trying to depose their leaders, he reminded doubters that even though Jesus had not returned when they expected, they needed to have faith that he would come at a future time. The letter is an insight into the state of the Corinthians found nowhere else.

Several other pieces of highly regarded literature, such as the *Second Letter of Clement*, are attributed to him. However, there is some debate over how much was written by his own hand. He is also historically credited with distributing the Apostolic Constitution, a draft previously said to have been written by the apostles. (It is now believed to have been written around 380 AD, almost two hundred years after the last of the original apostles died, and could not have been around in Clement's lifetime).

Even though Clement is believed to have been a leader in the Roman congregation at the end of the first century, it seems he was a popular figure far and wide.[63] That didn't change much after his death. Though none of his writings are included in the Bible, third and fourth-century Christians regarded his works so highly that they viewed them as scripture.

As alluded to previously, tradition has it that Clement's death was positively legendary. After Clement had converted hundreds of notable people, an angry Emperor Trajan banished him far from Rome—all the way to the Crimea. Clement was undeterred and continued his ministry there, performing miracles and converting hundreds more to Christianity. Word of Clement's doings got back to Trajan, and he ordered Clement's death. Under the emperor's command, Clement was put on a boat that set out on the Black Sea. Away from land, an anchor was tied to his body, and he was thrown overboard, dying a martyr's death.

---

[62] His only surviving work

[63] He is sometimes called a bishop of Rome, and some refer to him as the third pope. However, the early Christians didn't have a distinct clergy class. Each early Christian congregation was led by a group of older men or elders, not just one man. It wasn't until later that the hierarchal system of bishops and popes was used.

As sensational as the story is, it is also almost certainly untrue. Early biographers Eusebius and Jerome never mentioned any of this. Most sources say he died a more low-key death of natural causes while in exile. Though Clement was sainted by the Catholic Church and identified throughout history with an anchor symbol, the Catholic Encyclopedia notes that the first time the story appeared was hundreds of years after his death.

He wasn't the only famous Clement of early Christendom's history. Around the same time lived Clement of Alexandria, a theologian and philosopher who boasted Origen as one of his students. Not much is known about his personal life except that he was born to pagan parents, was probably married, and converted to Christianity. But why did he leave the religious beliefs of his birth, especially when he seemed to have extensive knowledge of Greek mythology and other mystical faiths?

Early in his life, Clement was turned off to pagan beliefs due to what he considered the shocking lack of morals within the religion, particularly among the Greek gods. This sent him on a journey to find beliefs he could agree with—wandering through Asia Minor, Palestine, Greece, and Egypt, searching for answers.

It was in Alexandria that Clement finally found his mentor in Christian studies, Pantaenus. Clement took up the battle against Gnostic teachings and, like his mentor, based his thinking and teachings on both the Bible and philosophy. Although philosophy had been creeping its way into Christian beliefs, Clement was the most influenced by Greek thinking via the works of Plato and the Stoics. He is said to have solidified the marriage of Christian religious beliefs with Greek philosophical concepts, effectively "Hellenizing" Christianity.

Considered the most educated and knowledgeable of the Church Fathers of his time, the scholarly Clement proposed there were three steps to reaching the peak of knowledge: science, philosophy, and Christian teachings. His thoughts on politics and economics and efforts to corral contemporary Christians into aligning their lives with gospel teachings are a big part of his legacy.

Clement of Alexandria wore many hats, so to speak: defender of Christianity (also known as an Apologist) controversial debater (polemicist) discourse writer, and missionary to intellectuals and the Greeks. When Pantaenus quit as head of his religious school, Clement took over until fleeing town to avoid the persecution brought on by

Roman Emperor Severus. The school was taken over by his most gifted student, Origen.

Clement never returned to Alexandria, dying in Palestine in the early third century. Some Christian sects later declared Clement a saint, but his martyrdom was revoked in the fifteenth century due to his sometimes-heretical writings and teachings.

"How can I blaspheme my King who has saved me?" The eighty-six-year-old man who uttered these words had lived a life that backed them up. Likely the last surviving link to the apostles, Polycarp had learned much from the beloved apostle John and others who knew Jesus.

Born in Smyrna, Turkey, Polycarp grew up to become a cherished overseer in the congregation there. Materially poor, the Smyrna congregation was at one time complimented for being spiritually rich. Polycarp assisted the congregation amidst a climate of hostility and hatred against them, pagan practices around them, and heated pressure to worship Roman gods.

Polycarp's notable kindness, generosity, self-sacrificing spirit, and love for the scriptures made him a beloved figure. So, when he wrote a letter of counsel to the Philippian congregation (*Epistle of Polycarp to the Philippians*), they undoubtedly paid attention to his words. Quoting numerous New Testament scriptures, many of them the words of Paul, Polycarp warned them about the love of money and other practices that were not approved by God, urged them to be zealous in doing good, reminded wives to love their husbands, and encouraged congregation elders to treat those under their care with compassion and mercy.

That didn't mean Polycarp didn't have enemies, including powerful Roman authorities. Near the end of his life, Polycarp escaped the enemies who wanted him captured, but only for a while. When the police and horsemen were led to his farm cottage hideout, he did not resist arrest but asked to pray before being taken away. It was said that his faith and demeanor caused the arresting officers to regret what they had to do.

When he said the words stated earlier, he was standing in the middle of an arena facing the Roman governor Statius Quadratus, surrounded by a hostile mob calling for his life. His offense? Refusing to worship their gods and discouraging others from doing so, as well. Ironically, they called him godless for sticking to his Christian beliefs. The governor approached Polycarp with an ultimatum: recognize the "genius" of

Caesar and announce "away with atheists" or pay with his life. Looking around at the pagan crowd, he said the words with conviction, albeit with a different meaning than what Caesar had in mind. The governor, however, was not satisfied. Pressing the elderly man further, he urged him to take an oath to renounce his faith. The older man remained steadfast in his determination, uttering his famous words.

After Polycarp's continued refusal to meet the governor's demands, preparations were made for his execution. The crowds gathered firewood, and although it was the Sabbath, hostile Jews in the stadium were very eager to help. Wood was piled up at the stake, and death by fire was set to take place. Alleged eyewitness accounts say that before he died, Polycarp tried to prevent any kind of worship or reverence to his body after death. Yet those who claimed his remains considered his bones "more precious than jewels or gold."

A living legacy that Polycarp left behind was his student and fellow Smyrnaean, Irenaeus. Although not much is known about Irenaeus' personal life beyond his Christian upbringing on the Aegean coast, he left a powerful testimony to the accuracy of the four Gospels.

During Irenaeus' lifetime, the New and Old Testament were developed. Not everyone agreed with which books should be in the canon, mainly because many works claimed they should be included as scripture. But only a few generations removed from Jesus and the apostles, Irenaeus put unshakable faith in the accuracy and divine nature of the Gospels, asserting that all four were indeed written by the men bearing their names. For this, he attested that they belonged in the biblical canon.

But it wasn't just the Gospels that he found essential to faith. Irenaeus emphasized the importance of many of Paul's teachings (namely his letters), especially regarding salvation. More than that, he believed in the validity of the Hebrew Scriptures/Old Testament and promoted the importance of the two parts of the Bible.

The Gnostics, on the other hand, did not put stock in the Hebrew Scriptures. Irenaeus' most well-known work, *Against Heresies,* was a targeted tearing down of Gnostic thinking. He did not buy into their idea of special knowledge. Instead, he steadfastly proclaimed salvation through real knowledge of the Christ. He used the scriptures to expose their false doctrines and show that what they taught had no merit according to the biblical canon.

At some point, Irenaeus moved to Lyons (in modern-day France). He narrowly escaped intense persecution and probable death when Emperor Marcus Aurelius sanctioned the mass killing of Christians in his city. Thanks to a letter he wrote and was personally delivering to Rome, Irenaeus was out of town when things went awry. However, many in Lyons did not escape the persecution. So, when he returned, he was given a leadership position in the congregation there. Though undoubtedly busy with these duties, he never stopped combating the Gnostics and other heretical groups, continuing to write *Proof of Apostolic Preaching* and other works.

There is no evidence regarding the reality of Irenaeus' death, only legend. In the sixth century, Gregory of Tours talked about his death during persecution, alongside many other converts. Perhaps because of this, he went down in history as a martyr, but the real truth of his death remains as mysterious as his personal life.

Irenaeus' death was not the end of his legacy, though. He heavily influenced the next generation, which included famous names like Tertullian and Hippolytus.

Hippolytus, a leader of the congregation in Rome around 199-217 AD, was a very busy writer—partly because he had a lot to write about. Disgusted by heretical and pagan teachings creeping into Christian doctrine, he wrote a large body of work called *Refutation of All Heresies*—a compilation of ten books. He wrote about the Christ, the Antichrist, the prophecies of Daniel, and church law. His *Apostolic Traditions* gives an insightful look into what rites were used in Rome during his time. But the most famous part of that larger body of work, *Philosophumena,* challenged the Trinity teachings.

Despite his close connection with Rome, Hippolytus' attitude toward the church was already souring over his disagreement about Trinity teachings. It soured even further when he was passed up for leadership in favor of Calixtus. His disagreement with the Roman leader was taken to new heights when he was scandalized by Calixtus' decision to pardon grave sins such as adultery. His high moral sense offended, Hippolytus split from Rome and became the leader of a breakaway group. A schism broke wide open in Rome, two leaders opposing one another. This move had him labeled in history as the first "antipope."

Hippolytus' death was also the stuff of legends. Roman poet Prudentius drew a parallel between the second-century Hippolytus and the mythological Hippolytus, son of the Greek Theseus, who died being dragged by wild horses.[64] Prudentius claims that the historical Hippolytus suffered the same gruesome death as a martyr. Although it is more likely he died from being forced to do hard labor in a mine, Hippolytus is still associated with horses in modern times.

The other person highly influenced by Irenaeus was Tertullian, a prolific historian of Christianity in his era. He was also one of the most well-known and biting Christian writers in history. His witty yet withering commentary and his often-paradoxical statements had people saying he was "incapable of being dull."

The highly educated son of a Roman centurion, Tertullian was one of the best lawyers in Rome. When he became a Christian in 193 AD, he devoted himself to a whole new type of defense—defending his spiritual beliefs. No one knows the circumstances of his conversion, but apparently Christians dying for their faith attracted his attention. However, it was not long before he became disenchanted with the version of Christianity he saw around him. The poor spiritual condition he witnessed had him leaving behind his original congregation and fleeing to Montanism—a sect that was highly devoted to prophecy and strict, no-frills lifestyles.

Many of Tertullian's logical arguments, observations, and thoughts are still quoted today, one of which is "Those who flee live to fight another day." Though considered genius-level brilliant, Tertullian also made some head-scratchingly odd statements, such as: "God is great when he is small," "The Son of God died: it is *immediately* credible— because it is silly," and "[Jesus] was buried, and rose again; the fact is certain —because it is impossible."

No one was safe from Tertullian's blistering pen. In one instance, he called a woman "the doorway of the devil." Of those who mixed secular beliefs with Christianity, he asked, "What has Athens to do with Jerusalem?" To Christians who attended pagan entertainment, he said, "How monstrous it is to go from God's church to the devil's—from the sky to the stye." And regarding self-centered people, he said, "He who lives only to benefit himself confers on the world a benefit when he dies." He did not leave out the pagans, mocking them and their ritual sacrifices.

---

[64] Hippolytus in Greek means "loose horse."

It was against the backdrop of Christians being vilified through superstitious and irrational reasoning that Tertullian came to their defense with his famous *Apology*. In this literary work, he notes with flair and wryness, "[Opposers] consider that the Christians are the cause of every public calamity and every misfortune of the people... If the Nile does not rise to the fields, if the weather will not change, if there is an earthquake, a famine, a plague—straightway the cry is heard: 'Toss the Christians to the lion!'" He tried to show that Christians were good, law-abiding citizens, and when they were executed for their faith, it was a loss to the world. He also pointed out that, although Christians were often considered traitors against the state, when several attempted government coups went down, the Christians were nowhere to be found among the treasonous.

But Tertullian's writings had a point beyond just a scathing take on what was happening at the time. His intention was to defend church doctrine, but in the end, he at times corrupted it. Though he condemned Christians for adopting Greek concepts and philosophy, the "doctrines of men and demons," he used them when it suited.

During his time, the relationship between God and Jesus had become confused, especially among previously polytheistic Greeks who did not grasp the concept of a single Almighty God and Jesus as the Messiah. When theologian Praxeas offered an explanation, Tertullian jumped to counteract Praxeas' teaching [65] with his essay *Against Praxeas*. Considering Praxeas a corruptor from the devil, Tertullian used the scriptures to reason that God and Jesus were separate beings. Yet later, in true Tertullian paradoxical style, he presented the idea that God, Jesus, and the Holy Spirit were three distinct beings existing as one divinity that "could not be divided." This theory, considered by some to be one of his biggest contributions to Christendom, laid the framework for the Trinity doctrine later debated by the fourth-century Council of Nicaea.

Unlike some of his fellow theologians, Tertullian lived to old age, dying in 225 AD. The details of his death appear to be lost to history, but much of his work has lived on for almost 1,800 years.

---

[65] His teaching was known as Modalism, which basically taught that God was different versions of himself at different times- the Father as creator, the savior as Jesus, and the Holy Spirit after Jesus' ascension to heaven.

Famous moralist writers like Jerome and Justin Martyr preached the value of living an ethical life, but after their deaths, one man took things to a new level. Born in mid-300s Turkey, Basil the Great was one of ten children in a large, wealthy, religious family. One might think that with a moniker like "great" he stood out at home, but there was competition over who was the most pious in the family. Both his parents, his grandmother, two of his sisters, and two of his brothers were all declared saints by the church.

Basil's life wasn't always one of strict piety—he spent time as a teacher and lawyer. But after meeting a monk, Eustathius of Sebaste, things took a dramatic turn for Basil. Realizing he needed to be fully devoted to God, he wrote that he had "wasted much time on follies and spent nearly all of (his) youth in vain labors." After the encounter, he felt his eyes were opened, proclaiming, "Suddenly, I awoke as out of a deep sleep. I beheld the wonderful light of the Gospel truth, and I recognized the nothingness of the wisdom of the princes of this world."

Deciding to adopt a life of extreme piety, Basil apprenticed himself to famous hermit monks. But unlike them, he did not completely give up secular life. He opened a school in Caesarea and once again practiced law. Even so, he still was devoted to his austere life. He didn't just write about prayer and monastic community life but helped set its guidelines. [66][67] He also formed and lived in a monastic community that included some of his family members. For that, Basil was dubbed one of the fathers of communal monasticism. However, the extreme austerity of monastic life didn't sit well with Basil, so he got to work reforming the rules of monastery life. Instead of making stricter rules, Basil moderated them, loosening up the austerity and campaigning for a more balanced approach.

Basil was considered a reformer. Well-known for helping the poor, he also wrote a sermon about caring for others' physical needs as if they were your own. He wrote more than just sermons, though. His large body of work covers work-life balance, material wealth, doctrine, morality, prayer, and observations on nature, to name a few.

---

[66] Relating to monks, nuns, and those who took religious vows. At first, many lived as hermits, but later, they formed communities and built monasteries.

[67] His liturgy, *The Diving Liturgy of Saint Basil the Great*, is still used in Eastern Catholic and Orthodox churches on feast days.

But perhaps Basil's most famous contribution was his support of the Trinity doctrine as outlined in the Nicene Creed. At that time, doctrine around the Trinity was under fierce debate. However, his heavy influence in religious and political spheres carried a lot of weight for his side of the issue. Even so, the debate raged on for years. (The Nicene Creed was modified several times over the centuries.) But Basil did not live to see the end result. Ironically, his excessively ascetic lifestyle hastened his demise, along with liver disease.

Many, many men shifted, reshaped, and remolded Christianity after the death of the apostles and into the first three centuries. Space will not allow us to mention all, but the collective influence of these men is seen throughout modern-day Christendom.

However, it was not just men who were devout in their faith or left their mark on history. Many women of the Bible and the first few centuries have also left their stories. Who were these women, and how did they make it into history?

Chapter 9: Women of Christianity

"Greetings, you highly favored one." How those words from an unknown man must have startled the ordinary, unmarried Jewish girl.[68] But this is how the angel Gabriel greeted Mary, perhaps the most well-recognized woman in Christian history. Gabriel was about to deliver the most shocking news—news that changed the life of Mary, her fiancé Joseph, and the world. It would also give her the most unique distinction in history.

The Gospels, however, don't give many details about Mary, particularly during Jesus' ministry. Despite being traditionally referred to as the Virgin Mary, Jesus' mother lived a fairly normal life after his birth. It was customary for Jewish couples to have large families, and Mary and Joseph were no exception. All four Gospels and the book of Acts either allude to this (calling Jesus Mary's firstborn) or directly discuss Mary's other children. Mark mentions four sons by name and also references their sisters. Mary must have spent much of her life as a busy wife and mother. She remained in Nazareth during Jesus' lifetime, probably unable to travel with her son as he and his disciples spread the divine message.

Sadly, though, she likely spent many years of her life without her husband. The last time Joseph is mentioned is fairly early in Jesus' life—when he is just twelve. Though the Gospels never mention what became

---

[68] Historians speculate she was around 15 or 16 years old at the time, but there are no historical records confirming her age.

of Joseph, it is presumed Mary became a widow at some point during Jesus' life. When she helps out at the wedding in Cana, Joseph is nowhere to be seen. Just before Jesus dies, he tells his apostle and close friend John to make sure his mother is taken care of.[69] Would he have needed to do that if Joseph were alive? Unlikely.

Mary was not sheltered from loss and hardship, losing her husband and then watching her firstborn son die an agonizingly cruel death as an alleged criminal. It's hard to imagine the depth of that type of grief. But after Jesus died, not much is known about what happened to Mary.

Though she had obviously been a very faithful Jewess, it is apparent that Mary listened to and accepted her son's message. She is mentioned in Acts as gathering for worship with the apostles in Jerusalem around Pentecost in 33 CE along with her sons, who also became believers after the death of their brother. In context, it seems she was on the ground floor of the first Christian congregation right as it was forming. However, this is the last time we see Mary mentioned in the scriptures.

Details of how she spent her last years and how and when she died are not in any Bible accounts, and there are very few historical records that say what happened. Apocryphal accounts like that of Hippolytus of Thebes in the seventh/eighth century say she didn't live very long after Jesus' death, with varying reports putting her death somewhere between 41-48 AD. Where she died is also a big question mark. Some scholars believe she died in Jerusalem, while other church traditions hold that she moved to Ephesus in Turkey and died there in her home.

As important as Mary's role was in early Christianity, she was not the only Mary in Jesus' life. Mary Magdalene stood next to Jesus' mother at his crucifixion, lending support to her dear friends during such a tragic time. Though a faithful believer in Jesus and a close friend of the family, Mary has often gone down in history for a more infamous reason—her alleged former profession as a prostitute. But was she?

Luke 7 tells about a woman, a "sinner" (thought to be a prostitute) who found out where Jesus was dining one day and went into the home to see him. Moved by his compassion and mercy, she rubbed very expensive perfumed oil on his feet. Crying, her tears fell onto his feet

---

[69] Before his death, Jesus' brothers had not yet accepted his teachings. Jesus likely wanted to entrust his mother to someone who shared her faith in him as the Messiah and would care for her spiritually.

and mixed with the oil. In a very caring gesture, she used her own hair to wipe away the tears and excess oil. Nothing in the Bible indicates who that woman is for certain, but Origen and other early Christian writers did not identify her as Mary Magdalene. Centuries after Mary Magdalene died, a prominent clergyman claimed she was the sinner of this account. She was, however, known among the disciples for a different reason—one that involved demons.

Luke mentions that she had been afflicted by not one or two but *seven* demons. Jesus had been the one to release her from their possession and a life of tortured misery. It is not surprising, then, that she showed her faith and appreciation for what he did by supporting him and the disciples as they traveled and preached.

Mary did have a distinct privilege mentioned by the apostle John. He relates that while Mary was weeping at Jesus' empty tomb, she was approached by two angels who asked why she was crying. After telling them that she was grieved because Jesus' body had disappeared, she turned around to see another man standing behind her. Thinking he was the gardener, she asked if he knew where Jesus' body would be. The stranger called her name, and the voice was familiar. The light of realization struck her —the man was not a gardener but Jesus himself. Mary Magdalene was the first person the resurrected Jesus appeared to after his death—even before the apostles. During their brief interaction, Mary, who literally clung to Jesus for fear he would be raised up to heaven right then and there, was tasked with telling the apostles and disciples that he had risen. For this, some churches have dubbed her an "apostle to the apostles."

Many rumors have swirled around Mary Magdalene over the centuries, some of which have landed her in infamy. One apocryphal book claims there was tension between Mary and the apostles, particularly Peter, due to jealousy over a vision. But perhaps one of the most controversial claims is that she was secretly married to Jesus. As fascinating as a secret romance might be, there is no evidence to support it. Mary Magdalene accompanied and supported Jesus and the disciples during their ministry, but she wasn't the only one. Several other women are mentioned for their supporting roles. Some of them married, but none are mentioned as his wife, including Mary.

But that's not the only rumor surrounding Mary's love life, nor was Jesus the only man she has been linked to in legend. Medieval legend places her as the apostle John's wife, possibly based on some church traditions that say she accompanied him to Ephesus, where she later died. The French might argue that. Their tradition has it that she went on a preaching mission to Provence in southern France and died there after living thirty years in a mountain cave.

But there was yet another Mary that was close to Jesus. Tears streaming down her face, in her grieved state she fell at Jesus' feet and declared, "Lord, if you had been here, my brother would not have died." A few days earlier, she and her sister Martha had sent word to Jesus that their brother Lazarus, his close friend, was very ill. Yet Jesus did not reach them for a few days, and by that time, the sisters were mourning the death of their beloved brother. Their grief was so potent that Jesus himself began to cry with them. Yet, just minutes later, Mary and Martha had their brother Lazarus returned to them through a miracle.

It was obvious by Mary and Martha's statements during this incident that they had tremendous faith in Jesus. But it was more than just that. Mary and her siblings were close friends with Jesus, often hosting him in their home. One of those visits was recorded in the Bible, giving a glimpse into the personalities of both sisters.

Martha was very hospitable and concerned for the needs of her guests in the tradition of good hostesses of her culture. With no one helping, she ran around the house making food and preparing everything for her guests. She stopped, annoyed, when she saw her sister sitting at Jesus' feet, listening to him. Frustrated, she complained to Jesus about her sister's lack of help. Jesus, however, reassured her that she didn't have to frantically prepare a lot of dishes and that Mary had made the wiser choice in listening to him teach.

The "sinner" or prostitute was not the only one mentioned as putting perfumed oil on Jesus. On a separate occasion, this Mary did, as well. She took a very expensive perfumed nard, one that cost about a year's salary, and poured it on Jesus' head and feet. This shows that her family was probably somewhat well off and that they valued Jesus and things with spiritual meaning more than material possessions. What's more, they had a life rich with good friends and tight family bonds.

The history of women in Christianity is not just limited to the Gospels. Priscilla worked hard. As refugees from the persecution of Emperor Claudius around 40 AD Rome, she and her husband Aquila fled to Corinth.[70] While there, the apostle Paul called them his "fellow workers in Christ." But they were more than that to him. At times, they all worked together, making tents to support themselves and their ministry.

When Paul went to Ephesus, Priscilla and Aquila went with him. There, Priscilla showed she had rock-solid faith. Both she and Aquila are noted as helping to correct and explain "the way of God" to a well-versed man named Apollos.

Priscilla showed that courage was not just a trait of her husband and that being a Christian (especially one associated with a controversial figure like Paul) was risky business. In his letter to the Romans, Paul mentions that they both "risked their necks" for his sake. Did they save his life in some way? There are no details given about what might have occurred, but it was something big enough that congregations in different countries were grateful to them for it. Despite the risks they took, they could not save Paul in the end. However, they maintained a friendship with him until his death, a friendship he cherished.

Priscilla is mentioned six times in the Bible, always mentioned together with Aquila. Likely, they had a strong bond as they worked and worshipped together. Tradition has it that they both died together as martyrs, though that might be a romanticized notion of what happened. Early historians only mention Aquila as being executed for his faith, while Priscilla's ultimate fate is left a mystery of history.

Many women are mentioned in the Gospels, the book of Acts, and the epistles—more Marys, the Samaritan woman at the well, Joanna, Susanna, Lydia, Tabitha, and others. A whole book could be written on the women who were on the ground floor of Christianity, but some of the most epic stories of martyrdom involve later Christian women.

Catherine of Alexandria is one venerated and sainted by certain churches. According to legendary accounts, the noble and intelligent Catherine went head-to-head with Emperor Maximinus over his violent persecution of Christians. She didn't stop there. Catherine also pointed out how bad it was to worship the false gods the Romans cherished. Unable to combat her cleverness on his own, the emperor called in scholars and philosophers to debate with the young woman. However,

---

[70] The imperial order forced Jews to leave Rome. Though they had converted to Christianity, as natural-born Jews, the order still applied.

they, too, were stumped by her witty and intelligent reasoning. So compelling was her speech that several of those who came to debate her were converted to Christianity on the spot. Those instant conversions led to their instant deaths.

As for Catherine, the enraged emperor had her whipped and thrown into prison. His empress, Valeria, was curious about Catherine and visited her in prison. She and her entourage of 200 were also immediately swayed by Catherine and got baptized. However, being part of the emperor's household did not save them from the sword, and they, too, were killed for their faith.

Having enough of her, Maximinus ordered that Catherine be executed on a spiked wheel—a terrible instrument of torture. But when she was brought to the wheel and touched it, the device crumbled to dust. In a rage, the emperor had her beheaded, and she died a martyr.

As fascinating as the story is, it was not part of the early Christian canon. Nothing was written about her before the ninth century, and many scholars doubt she was an actual person. If she was, her story is believed to be far more fiction than fact. However, there is a chance her story is based on a real person. Some scholars believe her story echoes that of the maiden Dorothea of Alexandria; others think she was based on the Greek philosopher Hypatia. In the 300s, Eusebius also wrote about a young woman called to the emperor to be his mistress. Upon refusing him, she had all her wealth stripped and was banished. But Eusebius never mentioned a name, so it remains uncertain whether she was the basis for Catherine's tale.

Saint Catherine of Alexandria, 1598-99.
Caravaggio, CC0, via Wikimedia Commons;
https://commons.wikimedia.org/wiki/File:Caravaggio_-_Saint_Catherine_of_Alexandria_(post-restoration_image).jpg

Catherine's story is not the only one of its kind to have made it into the halls of Christian history. Barbara (known as the Great Martyr in some churches) and Agnes of Rome were also young virgins who were said to face horrifying deaths unless they renounced their faith.

The "princess in the tower" legend of the beautiful Barbara is said to have started in fourth-century Nicomedia, Turkey. Her pagan father, a wealthy and prominent man, had extreme paternal jealousy over his beloved daughter. Worried about her virginity, he kept her imprisoned in a tower so that her beauty might not tempt her or any man to violate her chastity. Although she was kept from the outside world, her father lavished her with luxuries so that she lacked nothing materially.

Sitting in her gilded prison, she contemplated the gospel teachings that had reached her via her tutor. The more she learned and meditated on the beauty of the natural world outside her window, the more she was convinced that what she had been taught was true.

This, however, did not go over well with her father. On his return from a trip abroad, Barbara broke the news to him: she had become a Christian. Enraged, he demanded that she renounce her faith.

When she refused, the persecution mounted quickly. Her father began heaping abuses on her in the hope that he could pressure her into recanting—all to no avail. Barbara remained firm in her stance, even as she faced torture and death.

Seeing that he was getting nowhere, Barbara's father turned her over to the governor, her only crime being her faith. Despite being subjected to extreme physical torments, Barbara was said to have some help from above. Torch fire could not come near her skin without being miraculously extinguished, and angels healed her wounds every night.

After enduring cruel tortures, Barbara was handed her death sentence: beheading. Even worse, the sentence was to be carried out by her own father, who would rather she die than be a Christian.

Statue of Barbara.
https://www.metmuseum.org/art/collection/search/470617

There are several versions of the story, one involving betrayal by a shepherd who was turned into a marble statue for his treachery. In another version, when her father grabs her hair and raises his sword to strike the fatal blow, Barbara's long hair bursts into flames. Her father survives the spontaneous hair combustion but cannot escape punishment for killing his daughter. He is struck by lightning and consumed by flames on his way home.

No version of her story is found before the seventh century, but she began to be worshipped as a saint a few centuries later, invoked as protection against lightning. Despite being venerated by some in modern times, Catherine's absence in authentic early Christian writings raises serious doubts about whether she existed, and some churches have removed her from their list of saints. Still, her story has made her a popular figure in many churches today.

Then there is Agnes, another beauty and perhaps the youngest of the legendary women. A tender twelve years old in 304 AD, when legend has it she was martyred, Agnes became a symbol of purity and chastity. During her short life, Christianity was declared a cult by the Roman Empire, and as was the case for others, being found out meant death—even if one was very young.

In one version, the noble-born Agnes learned about the Gospels from her nursemaid despite her pagan-believing parents. Not short on rich, young suitors, Agnes caught the particular attention of the governor's son. Despite showering her with precious jewels, he could not win her over as she declared that she was "already the spouse of a Lover much more noble and powerful than [him]."

Not taking the rejection well, the young man turned around and told his father that Agnes was a Christian. Brought in for questioning, she freely admitted it was true. She was then sent to the temple of Vesta, the Roman virgin goddess. Ordered to become a Vestal Virgin of the temple or at least offer a sacrifice, Agnes refused any pagan worship whatsoever. Since, by Roman law, virgins could not be executed, the judge ordered her to a more humiliating fate. Agnes was punished by being stripped naked and brought to a brothel. At the brothel, she had many gawkers, all of whom were so awed by her pure presence that they refused to touch her—except for one rather bold Roman youth. He dared try to violate her and, for his efforts, was struck blind by divine sources.

However, her end was the same as many of her fellow believers. In some versions, she is executed during a wave of persecution by Emperor Diocletian. In another more shocking version, she is declared a witch and set to be burned at the stake. Naked, she is tied up in front of onlookers. To protect her modesty, her hair miraculously grows long and flowing to cover her body. When the wood refuses to ignite, an officer goes in for the fatal blow, brutally stabbing or beheading her. The gruesome death of one so young is shocking even to the blood-lusting pagan Romans, and supposedly, this leads to some sympathy for the Christians.

Since the fourth century, many customs, traditions, and shrines have been dedicated to Agnes. Her tale has changed over the centuries. In some cases, the details of her life are limited to her age and the fact that she was executed. However, in the mid-fourth century, in the version told by Pope Damascus I, Agnes immediately outs herself as a Christian when the imperial edict against Christians is made. Describing her as courageous and modest, the account says she used her long hair to cover her body at the time of her death.

Her legendary modesty and chastity got her honored as a saint and a patron for virgins, young girls, engaged couples, and victims of sexual assault. She is honored by both Catholic and Orthodox churches down to today.

Whether these stories are the stuff of legends or authenticated, it is no myth that women suffered persecution for their faith along with their Christian brothers. Yet what motivated the Roman Empire to run down and execute people of a love and peace-based faith?

Agnes before her martyrdom. Painting by Jusepe de Ribera, 1641.
https://www.wikiart.org/en/jusepe-de-ribera/st-agnes-in-prison-1641

Chapter 10: Persecutions

Pagan worship, war and patriotism, violent and sensational entertainment—these were the things that enveloped the lives of many Romans. These were encouraged, if not almost mandatory, across the Roman Empire. The Romans did not particularly care what religion anyone practiced. In fact, they rarely persecuted anyone for their religion. They didn't care as long as everyone went along with the cultural crowd, so to speak—performing military service and sacrificing to the gods, including the emperor. Just one pinch of incense was all it took to stay alive, but the Christians refused to compromise their beliefs. This made them stand out as different and put a target on their backs.

It wasn't just their refusal to worship the ancestors, emperor, and gods of the empire that made Christians different. They actively spoke out against pagan beliefs and taught something that starkly contrasted with what the Romans held dear. Christians stood on their own in these areas and in their general behavior, favoring peace and love. They refused military service and condemned the depravity of Roman entertainment in the colosseums and amphitheaters.

In general, the persecution of Christians was nothing new. John the Baptist suffered beheading for confronting Herod, and Jesus said it was just the beginning. Paul also knew a thing or two about persecution. While the persecution of Christians in Roman territories was never empire-wide, some of the pockets of persecution that occurred were intense and terrifying. Starting in 64 AD, Nero ramped up the brutality to new levels, and its impacts on Christians were profound.

Nero

After the city of Rome burned that year, turmoil and unrest plagued the empire even more.[71] Many simplify the explanation for Nero's persecution of Christians, boiling it down to him needing a scapegoat for the disastrous fire. But in reality, it was more complex than that.

There was plenty of unrest in Nero's kingdom, and in his eyes, Christians presented another threat to the established order. Roman society had its hierarchies, but here came the Christians preaching that God was not partial based on status or background, and neither were they. They recognized the authority of God above all, rejecting the idea of Roman gods and the divinity of the emperor. Christians promoted the idea that all humans were equal in God's eyes—not an appealing idea to someone who held himself above the rest.

Although Christians were generally peaceful and law-abiding, to an already suspicious ruler, the ideology and swift growth of the movement could have raised the alarm regarding another potential rebellion on his hands. Especially troubling to Nero was that some of the newly baptized Christians were in positions of authority and/or had considerable influence among their communities. In his opinion, this increased the threat.

According to the historian Tacitus, Christians faced mass executions for what Nero and Roman society labeled "hating the human race." As such, they deserved horrific deaths that, in many cases, became a matter of sport.

Nero's reaction to this perceived threat was absolutely brutal and humiliatingly public. He staged spectacles where blood-lusting crowds gathered to watch Christians covered in animal skins and chased by vicious dogs or torn to shreds by fierce animals. Others were crucified in the common way Romans executed criminals, while others faced an even worse fate. Tied to stakes and covered in tar, they were set on fire and used to light the roads at night. Nero himself used these human torches as ghastly nightlights to line his spectacular gardens.

Nero's torture of the Christians was so appalling that it garnered sympathy from ordinary citizens who saw what was happening. But public outrage wasn't going to change Nero's mind, and the people were

---

[71] Historian Tacitus wrote that Nero started the fire, but some modern scholars dispute that claim.

told that the Christians' capital punishment was for the ultimate good of the empire. Yes, this was only the beginning of the 250 years of uncertainty and persecution faced by those who professed to be Christians.

Domitian

As appalling as Nero's tortures were, it was his successor, Domitian, who was dubbed the "beast from hell who sat in its den, licking blood." Reveling in his own sense of unwavering divinity, he styled himself "God the Lord," "Lord of the Earth," and "Thou Alone" while pressing those around him to hail him as "Glory," "Holy," and "Invincible." Obviously, Christians would strongly disagree with his hearty sense of self, which was a problem for him.

Early Christian writers/historians Eusebius, Tertullian, and Melito all wrote about Domitian's slanders, accusations, persecutions, and cruelty against Christians. Irenaeus reported that he had the apostle John exiled to the island of Patmos. Other stories tell of Domitian's cousin and Roman consul Titus Flavius Clemens and his wife converting to Christianity and shortly thereafter being exiled and executed at Domitian's command.

But none of these stories came out during or remotely near the time they happened. Not until at least 300 years later did these stories begin to crop up. Among those circulating these stories, not one was a pagan author. With little evidence to go on, some modern archeologists have labeled Domitian's persecutions as fake news. There is plenty of evidence that he persecuted Jews—of that there is no doubt—but did he have it in for the Christians? At the time, Christians were not widely recognized as separate from the Jews, so could Domitian's persecutions of the Jews have enveloped some Christians as well?

The persecution of Christians under Emperor Domitian is up for debate, and there is a lot of speculation. Given what is known about several other Roman emperors and their feelings about Christians, it is not out of the realm of possibility or probability. However, there is definitive evidence of how his successor viewed the Christian movement.

Trajan

Though his predecessors appeared to lump the Christians in with the Jews, Trajan saw them through a different lens—one that made them a separate entity. He wasn't as antagonistic towards the Christians as Nero. He didn't bother to actively hunt them down and punish them, and he acknowledged they didn't commit any crimes. But the exchange between Governor Pliny the Younger and the emperor gives a clear view of Christianity under Trajan.

Pliny was stumped as to what to do. Several Christians had been dragged to court to be judged by the governor. Yet, he was not sure what the exact charges against them were; neither did he get a clear answer from those who charged them. As far as he could tell, they seemed harmless. None of them had committed a crime. Could he legally execute them just to get the matter over and done with? It seemed the best course. After all, they stubbornly and defiantly refused to recant their faith, which he had labeled a "contagion." Not only that, but the number of sacrifices in the city and the merchants who sold them were being affected: Christianity was not good for the pagan sacrifice business. Yes, execution was the safest route, but he just needed to check to ensure he did the right thing. So, Pliny wrote to the emperor for advice.

The emperor took a non-committal stance on the matter. He assured Pliny that he had done the right thing, but the emperor wasn't looking to actively pursue Christians. But if Pliny did find them in court, he was free to convict and punish any who refused to repent of their Christian ways. But some "Christians" who had come to Pliny's court were now former, having given up the faith. That in itself was no crime. As long as they had put their Christian days behind them and proved it through sacrificial incense to the gods, they were free to go about their lives. Pliny and Trajan were not the only ones to adopt a moderate stance regarding Christians. Trajan's successor, Marcus Aurelius, followed suit—at least at first.

Trajan.
https://commons.wikimedia.org/wiki/File:Traianus_Glyptothek_Munich_336.jpg

Marcus Aurelius

Marcus Aurelius' moderate stance was more an official one than a true reflection of his feelings. While Marcus Aurelius is considered one of the more benevolent and liberal emperors, not everyone around him was as open-minded. Trusted anti-Christian advisors got in his ear and convinced him that the peace-loving Christians were, in fact, quite a force of dangerous revolutionaries. And, to top that off, they were "grossly immoral" in their refusal to worship the gods. He became convinced that they were a danger to Roman society.

The greatest danger was perhaps not from the emperor himself but from the anti-Christian propaganda he encouraged and allowed to circulate. The result reported by later writers was one filled with horrifying tortures and gruesome deaths in a reign of terror. Among the victims of this wave of persecution were Irenaeus and Justin Martyr.

Yet, this extreme violence seems to be at odds with the emperor's character. Many modern scholars question the sensational reports of those who were not alive during this period. It also contradicts Tertullian's take on Aurelius, whom he called "our protector and patron." Tertullian also referenced letters from the emperor in which he claimed Christians in his army saved the troops from certain death through prayer. For that, Marcus Aurelius dissuaded others from exacting the death penalty on them, although he didn't change the punishment for practicing Christians.

So, the truth about persecution under Marcus Aurelius, though not totally understood, seems to lie somewhere in the middle. It is obvious by the death of two well-known Christian writers that terrible persecutions were heaped on the Christians during that time, but these were perhaps not directly sanctioned by Aurelius. A similar story unfolded during the reign of Severus.

Severus

Severus didn't have any particular grudge against the Christians. In fact, the nursemaid who took care of his son was a professed Christian. Still, this did not stop him from issuing an empire-wide law forbidding anyone from converting to Christianity (or Judaism, for that matter). That edict kicked off another wave of ferocious persecution that not even the skilled pen of Tertullian could combat. This time, the bulk of the action took place in North Africa.

During this time, Clement of Alexandria and Origen's father died. It was also when the martyr Perpetua penned her dramatic final memoir detailing her time in prison. Only twenty-two, she anxiously pined away for her baby, who was still breastfeeding. Eventually, she and her infant were reunited in her jail cell. Her pregnant servant/friend Felicitas was imprisoned along with her, giving birth in her dark cell at eight months pregnant. Perpetua details the indignities heaped on Felicitas while they awaited execution, along with some vivid dreams she had regarding what would happen. Her narrative ends the night before they are sent to the arena, but her story is picked up by another narrator, who continues their story. He tells how those about to go into the arena were forced to wear the robes and tunics of priests and priestesses of the gods, yet to the end Perpetua refused to compromise even in this last detail. For her faith, she and Felicitas were stripped naked, put in nets, and dragged into the arena. The crowd was put off by this, and the two were brought back and given simple tunics before returning to the arena floor. They and others were accosted by angry animals and, though injured, did not die. The bloodlust of the audience calling to be satiated, the survivors were brought back into the arena, where soldiers finished them with swords.

There is little doubt that Perpetua was a historical person. No matter how much of her story is true or embellished, it gives readers a glimpse into what professed Christians endured during this time.

However, with the end of Severus' life came the end of persecution—at least for the time being. Christians enjoyed fifty more years of peace before their troubles renewed.[72]

Decius

When persecution returned in 249 AD during the reign of Decius, it returned in a big way. With invading barbarian hordes and other troubles weakening the empire, Decius wanted to solve the problem by reinforcing the traditional worship of the gods. An edict commanding everyone in the empire to offer incense to the gods was an obvious problem for the Christians, and their refusal irritated Decius. After having prominent clergyman Fabian of Rome executed, Decius said he would take a "rival to the throne rather than another bishop of Rome." From this imperial aggravation stemmed the first empire-wide persecution of Christians, and it was intense. It also set a precedent for

---

[72] Though there was a brief period of turmoil during the three-year reign of Maximinus.

the emperors who followed.[73]

Valerian

When Emperor Valerian first took the throne of Rome, he was unbothered by the Christians and let them be for the most part. But as war, civil unrest, and plagues began to spiral out of control across the empire, Valerian needed a scapegoat. Taking a page out of Nero's playbook, he pinned Rome's problems on the Christians. Added to this was the manipulative persuasion of one of his anti-Christian generals, making the year 257 AD a turning point in his attitude. From then on, Valerian not only enforced Decius' policies but increased their intensity.

As under Decius, Rome's "religious tolerance" showed in the fact that the emperors didn't care that Christians practiced their faith so long as they also observed Roman forms of worship. In his new edicts, Valerian demanded that all Christian clergy members sacrifice to the gods or face an agonizing death. Valerian followed through on his word.

Numerous clergymen across the empire, including prominent men like Sixtus and Cyprian, were executed. Barbarity reigned in many cases, such as that of Saturninus of Toulouse. After being subjected to horrific indignities, he at last had his feet bound and tied to the tail of an angry bull. The animal was let loose to rampage down the temple steps with the unfortunate clergymen bouncing and dragging behind until his head was crushed.

In Utica, 300 Christians were gathered and placed around a burning kiln. After refusing an order to sacrifice to Jupiter, all 300 were sacrificed in the kiln. This burning alive was by no means an isolated incident. As far away as Spain, prominent clergymen were set on fire.

Others, including devout women, had tigers and other fierce animals unleashed on them. Some endured unimaginable ordeals—first scourged with whips before being strung up on the gallows. Yet, they were not allowed to die. After they were taken down, their skin was burned with chemical lime before they were roasted over flames and then finally beheaded.

Those of the higher class who escaped gruesome deaths had their property stripped from them by the state. The more unfortunate Christian servants of the imperial household were shackled and sent off

---

[73] Until this point, persecutions were in localized pockets instead of empire-wide.

to slave away in Roman mines.

Towards the end of his reign, Valerian was captured by the Persians during a war and suffered a fate similar to the one he imposed on Christians. When his son Gallienus took over, he had a far more sympathetic outlook on the Christians, reversing his father's policies and even restoring confiscated property. Things remained relatively safe for the Christians for several more emperors until Diocletian took the reins of Rome.

Diocletian

Despite the fact that his wife was a Christian, Diocletian went all-out in resurrecting the persecution against Christians. He wasn't just satisfied to have Christians sacrifice to the gods; he was going for complete extermination of the entire religion. This fiercest onslaught began what became known as The Great Persecution.

Diocletian had tolerated Christianity for many years, but like other rulers before him, he was looking for a way to stabilize the tumultuous empire. So, he turned to creating uniformity by enforcing Roman religious rites. And again, Christian refusal was taken as a disruption to the peace and morality of the empire.

Once more, an anti-Christian advisor helped an emperor become more inflamed against the Christians. All Christian worship was utterly forbidden by imperial decree. This included the destruction of places of worship and Christian literature and the arrest of any Christian who didn't wholeheartedly perform an act of worship to the Roman gods. Not even the imperial household escaped the Christian purge, with the empress and their daughter also being swept up in the persecution.

In some regions, Christians fought back against the imperial order. Incensed by the violation of civil rights, a professed Christian named Nicomedia publicly destroyed a copy of the edict, earning him death by being burned alive.

In Phrygia, a small village inhabited entirely by Christians was burned to ash. Yet other persecutors took the time to refine their brutal punishments. Eusebius, alive at the time this was happening, wrote that Christians not executed or forced into the mines suffered perhaps even worse physical cruelty, having their eyes pulled from their sockets or feet hacked off from their legs.

However, not everyone was on board with this indiscriminate slaughter. Prominent community leaders like judges and other officials risked their lives to protect Christian family and friends. This stood in defiance of apostates and traitors who turned Christians over to authorities.

Galerius

After Diocletian abdicated the throne in 304 AD, his successor and son-in-law Galerius took up the torch of persecution. Though Diocletian had given the original orders, it was Galerius who earned the credit for instigating the persecution behind the scenes. Now in full command, he continued the ruthless campaign.

That campaign came to a screeching halt in 311 AD when Galerius became deathly ill. Inflicted with a gruesome and painful disease (possibly gangrene or intestinal cancer), Galerius quickly changed his tune. Fearing that his sickness was divine retribution from the fed-up Christian god, he was eager to appease. Galerius was willing to issue orders that undid his former edicts against the Christians—on one condition. The Christians needed to collectively pray for the emperor's health to be restored. Two years after falling ill, Galerius issued empire-wide edicts of full tolerance towards Christians. This time, Christians experienced lasting peace (for the most part) until the end of Roman power.

Yet the Roman emperors were not the only powerful rulers who affected the history of the Christian religion. What was life like under the declared Christian emperor Constantine the Great?

Chapter 11: Constantine's Contribution

In 311 AD, imperial letters were sent to all governors of the Roman Empire. Emperor Constantine and his co-emperor of the eastern provinces, Licinius, issued edicts reversing all previous restrictions against Christians. Far be it from him to interfere with anyone who wanted to "give their mind to the cult of Christianity" or any other cult, for that matter. In reality, Christians who had their property confiscated would not get everything back. But who was the real man behind this apparently benevolent order, and how exactly did he embrace Christianity?

As a young man, Constantine witnessed the violent and intrigue-filled imperial court of Emperor Diocletian. The execution of rivals and finger-pointing was an early education. When Diocletian murdered his way to the top, his first order of business was to divide the empire into what he called the Tetrarchy. There would now be two emperors (Augusti). One would rule the Eastern provinces and the other the Western. These would be helped out by their vice-emperors (caesares). This way, it would be far easier to manage borders and enemy attacks across the vast empire.

In the West, Augustus Maximian set up court in Milan, with Constantine's father, Constantius I Chlorus as his second in command. Constantine, however, stayed with Diocletian and served as a bodyguard before becoming an officer in the military.

An intelligent, energetic, and natural-born leader, Constantine made a habit of chatting up his troops, smartly gaining a rapport with his men and earning their loyalty. The young general was ambitious and driven to succeed at any cost—even that of someone else's life.

Besides being an outstanding general, Constantine excelled as an organizer and administrator. Throughout his life, he worked hard to learn as much as possible. He was also religious to the point of being superstitious and very emotional. Because he wanted to be popular, he was easily deceived and taken advantage of. He suffered from fits of anger brought about by a highly suspicious and jealous mind, occasionally resorting to murder.

When Constantine's father became one of the new Augusti in 305 AD, he was expected to make his son Caesar. Instead, Constantine was passed over in favor of more nepotistic choices that would make his co-Augustus Galerius happy. However, the men serving under Constantine were offended by this snub of their commander. They believed he should have rightfully been promoted.

When Constantius died the following year, the roller coaster of Constantine's promotions and demotions began in earnest. Constantine's troops saw an opportunity and tried to grasp it for their leader, declaring him the new Augustus. Galerius, however, put the brakes on Constantine's elevation to grand status, instead promoting Severus to Augustus and placing Constantine as his Caesar. Even though he had his troops behind him, Constantine did not believe he could fight Galerius and Severus on this, so he accepted the Caesar-ship and bided his time.

Retired Augustus Maximian and his son Maxentius were also not keen on Constantine's missed promotion, so they took it upon themselves to declare him Augustus. Severus and Galerius went to war with them over it, with disastrous consequences. Severus and Galerius' armies were defeated, and although Severus surrendered, he was executed. Struck with fear, Galerius turned and retreated.

A few years later, Galerius his nerve and again demoted Constantine to Caesar while promoting Licinius to Augustus. But Constantine wasn't having it this time. He refused the title change and resolutely went about as Augustus. Now there were three Augusti and only two parts of the empire, so Galerius had to make room for Licinius as ruler of the Illyrian provinces.

Just a few years after making Constantine ruler, Maximian lost favor with him. Shamed after being defeated in battle, Maximian took his own life. Maxentius stewed, viewing Constantine as the cause of his father's death. After his victory, Constantine ended the Tetrarchy and again put the kingdom under one allegedly rightful ruler—himself. Maxentius begged to differ. He had a much stronger hereditary claim to the throne. Eventually fighting broke out, culminating in the history-making Battle of the Milvian Bridge.

Safely secured behind the heavily fortified walls of Rome, Maxentius was feeling lucky. Thinking the omens were in his favor, he made an overconfident and ultimately catastrophic mistake in judgment. Leaving the city, he led his troops to confront Constantine head-on. However, there was one little problem—Maxentius had destroyed all the bridges across the Tiber River going to Rome, including the Milvian Bridge. Now needing to cross to meet up with Constantine's troops, Maxentius had his men make a pontoon bridge, placing their boats side by side across its width.

The armies clashed fiercely, and one of Maxentius' flanks was pushed back onto the makeshift boat bridge. The weight of the soldiers strained the boats until, overladen, they sank into the Tiber and took the men down with them. Maxentius was among the drowned, and his head was taken by Constantine's troops and proudly paraded in victory.

So, what does this obviously political fight have to do with Christianity? Eusebius and Constantine tell of a sensational event right before the battle—perhaps the turning point for the superstitious Constantine.

According to Constantine (and later written down by Eusebius), the noon sun was high in the sky the day before the battle. Looking up, he saw a "cross-shaped trophy" sitting over the sun. On the cross were etched the words "By this conquer." Constantine and his accompanying body of soldiers stood in amazement.

That night, he kept thinking about what the sign could mean when, finally, he was overtaken by sleep. Constantine claimed he was told in a dream to paint the mark of the Christ, an X, on the shields of his men. This mark was said to protect his men from enemy attack. It also inspired Constantine to create a jewel-encrusted gold lance (the man loved his jewels) on which hung a silk banner embroidered with a wreath bearing Christ's name.[74]

Yet it wasn't enough. Outside the gates of Rome, Constantine had the Sibylline Books brought to him so he could check what the oracles had to say. It was there he found the words he wanted to see: "On this day the enemy of the Romans will perish." Confident in all sorts of divine backing, he marched out to victory.

It is generally said that these incidents sparked Constantine's conversion to Christianity (though he was not baptized until right before his death). But did the man whose favorite gods were Mars and Apollo truly convert to Christianity, and what were his motives for doing so?

Constantine's conversion by Peter Paul Reubens.
https://commons.wikimedia.org/wiki/File:Constantine%27s_conversion.jpg

Like any good superstitious soldier, Constantine likely believed in covering his bases. In his mind, if he wanted to win politically and militarily, all the gods, regardless of religion, should be appeased to increase his chances of success. To mistakenly offend a god by leaving

---

[74] This banner, called a labarum, was always taken by Constantine on military exploits from that time forward and eventually became the symbol of the Byzantine Empire.

them out would be to risk divine retribution. For him, Christianity was less about Jesus' ransom sacrifice and more of a magic talisman for his victories.

Similarly, "conversion" didn't seem like a big deal to Constantine. He already worshipped the sun, so it was a small leap for him to worship the Son. In fact, he was the one who introduced Christmas, an event that melded sun worship with Son worship.

So, in 313 AD, Constantine made it official: not his conversion but the decriminalization of Christianity. The Edict of Milan allowed every citizen of the empire freedom of worship. Though Rome was usually tolerant of other religions, it was a radical move for the empire—a step that would take it from Christian persecutor to Christian patron.

But the perpetual pesky problem of a fractured empire plagued Constantine's reign. Like others before him, he sought religious unity as a way to hold the empire together. However, he couldn't just toss out hundreds of years of native pagan culture without consequence. After all, he had just granted religious freedom to Christians with an edict that technically allowed everyone else to worship as they pleased. So, how was he going to work this sticky problem out? By meshing together pagan and Christian beliefs, he hoped that the various peoples of the empire would unite in happy brotherhood. However, Christianity itself had become divided.

Two sects, the Donatists and Arians, were the main players at this time. The Donatists had a very strict view of holiness and were not keen on Roman emperors interfering in their godly affairs. They didn't approve of the way things were being run from the church in Rome either, causing a break from the main branch at the time. Saying that all other branches of Christianity were not worthy or holy enough did not win them any popularity among other professed Christians. An uproar ensued, and violent attacks were made on Donatist churches in North Africa.

The Arians, for their part, maintained the first-century beliefs about the divinity of Jesus. They refused to accept the now more common teachings that Jesus had supreme status as part of the Trinity. Rather, they held that he was created as an individual subject to God rather than equal to him. Although this teaching was original to Christianity, times had changed, and the idea created quite a stir. This became the main sticking point during the famed Council of Nicaea in 325. In the two years before that, Constantine had sent letters to the church, trying to get them more united. When that didn't work, he convened the council to have them work it out face-to-face.

Although not baptized, Constantine took part in the debate. Making his entrance into the council, Constantine was arrayed in all the splendor of his gold and purple attire, his jewels radiating their glow as he walked down the aisle in his imperial pomp. In Constantine's opening statement, it is apparent how much the internal strife among Christendom plagued him. In part, he stated: "For, in my judgment, internal strife within the Church of God is far more evil and dangerous than any kind of war or conflict, and these our differences appear to me more grievous than any outward trouble." He indicated he didn't think the matter was worthy of the debate it was causing and that it primarily arose from academically inclined clergymen having too much time on their hands. He encouraged those present to come to one conclusion on who Jesus was in relation to God.

Tired and in disagreement with the Arians, Constantine sided with the rest of Christendom on the matter. All but two of the clergymen gathered voted to accept Jesus as equal to God, and they wrote down a formal statement of belief (the Nicaean Creed) to seal it in writing. The council condemned the sect's leader, Arius, as dangerous and heretical. Arius was then excommunicated, and the emperor shipped him into exile (though he returned to good graces a few years later).

Within Christendom, the events in Nicaea are considered the pinnacle of Constantine's religious transformation. Yet another transformation would take place several years later. In 330 AD, Constantine moved the empire's capital to a little town on the Bosporus strait known as Augusta Antonina. Previous Emperor Septimius Severus had razed it, but Constantine came along to raise it back up and turn it into the "Queen of Cities." He renamed it Constantinople, and its gleaming wealth created the backdrop for a new epicenter of Christian intellectualism and culture.

Though he continued to phase Christianity into the empire, the emperor was still not baptized. What was the hang-up? He was certainly making changes to the Roman system—passing laws that tightened up morals and tried to prevent abuses, especially of a sexual nature.[75] There

---

[75] But sometimes these were savagely enforced. In some cases, moral crimes could lead to being

is ample evidence that he was strong in his convictions regarding his faith. He set himself up as a patron of Christians—commissioning new Bibles for congregations in Constantinople, favoring them with money for houses of worship (such as the original Hagia Sophia), doling out high-ranking positions, and exempting the clergy from taxes. If that weren't enough, he styled himself the head of the church and promoted unity within Christendom.

Though he certainly may have had some genuine conviction about what he learned, adopting Christianity wasn't without its perks for the emperor. Eusebius wrote in the emperor's biography that he "derived the source of imperial authority from above" and was "strong in the power of the sacred title." If he could claim divine backing for his imperial authority, well, that would put him in an advantageous position. After all, he believed his rise to power and success were linked to divine support.

The problem was, as he was helping Christians and attempting to bring the empire in line with Christian morality, his personal life left much to be desired. Temperamental, paranoid, megalomaniacal, cruel, violent, and prone to murder even within his own family, Constantine hadn't quite refined his Christian character, and he seemed to know it.

As emperor, he had blood on his hands from wars and other unsavory acts he may have considered necessary. But in his thinking (perhaps a common way of thinking at the time), as long as he wasn't baptized, he couldn't be condemned for any of those sins. His plan seemed to be to repent and be absolved of all prior sins at just the right moment, when he was at death's door and could commit no more transgressions. He was essentially aiming to go to his grave "sin-free." Eusebius' writings hint that perhaps the clergy were reluctant to allow his baptism for the ethical and moral reasons already stated. Either way, Constantine's baptism into Christianity didn't occur until seventeen days before his death, as he lay sick and in mortal peril. But to the very end, Constantine was a man who wanted to cover all his bases. The day before he died, he also offered a sacrifice to Zeus.[76]

When Constantine died in 337, Rome was still a mix of pagan and Christian worshippers. But as his legacy, he had legalized Christianity

---

burned alive or the offender having molten lead poured down their throat.

[76] He still held the title Pontifex Maximus (or supreme priest) of the pagan Roman religion.

and made it an officially recognized religion of the state, meaning Christians could now freely meet for worship without fear. But even though Constantine helped usher in a historically significant change and made Christianity a state religion, it would not become *the* state religion for another forty-three years. And in that time, many more branches would sprout.

Chapter 12: State Religion and Heresies

After Constantine, most emperors either embraced or, at the very least, tolerated Christianity, as it seemed good for the business of the empire. However, a hiccup in the path of Christianity becoming the official state religion came during the reign of Emperor Julian, starting in 361 AD. While much of the empire was changing from paganism to Christianity, Julian ran the opposite way. Having been taught Christian teachings, in part by Eusebius himself, Julian later preferred the classic Greek and Roman philosophies and deities, earning him the nickname Julian the Apostate. He didn't exactly re-criminalize Christianity; in fact, he was fine with the Donatists, who were busy fighting against corruption in the Roman church. He welcomed them back from the exile imposed on them by the previous emperor.[77] Still, he did make it a point to ban certain church rites and to harass Christians so they could not protest the empire's reintroduction to paganism.

In the grand scheme of things, Julian's bid to return to the paganist and philosophy-filled days didn't last long, and it hardly stemmed the tide of Christianity. Neither did it put the kingdom back together as one united empire as he had hoped.

---

[77] This came back to bite later emperors when the Donatists threw their support behind a rebellion of farmers who were angry over taxation.

In 380 AD, Emperor Theodosius I threw the full imperial weight of the state behind Christianity. After suffering a bout of illness, the newly baptized emperor issued the Edict of Thessalonica. This edict made Christianity the official religion of the empire. However, by this time, Christianity was far from one religion, and numerous sects were constantly contending for supremacy and squabbling over doctrine. The first council in Nicaea hadn't been enough to unify their beliefs. The debate between Nicene and Arian ideas of the Trinity continued to rage.[78]

Theodosius sought to end the controversy once and for all and, as many before him, sought to unify the empire through unified doctrine. The Archbishop of Constantinople, Gregory Nazianzus, was on the same page as the emperor. They called all of Western Christendom together for the First Council of Constantinople (the second ecumenical council). The council spent three months hammering out the details of the Trinity doctrine that had not been dealt with at Nicaea. Some argued for the divinity of the Holy Spirit, while others were not keen on the idea. Accusations flew, condemnations were made, and bishop titles were snatched away.

In all, seven canons were established, though only four were doctrinal. The other three dealt with procedures regarding the Bishop of Constantinople and what to do with certain heretics in the church.

The council also established the doctrine under the Nicene Creed, specifically the Trinity teaching, which they tweaked, to be the official dogma of the church (set in stone with the new Nicene-Constantinopolitan Creed). Turning a deaf ear to continued Arian protest, the church declared the following: (1) Jesus is God, (2) Jesus died and was resurrected, (3) others will also be resurrected from the dead, (4) the Holy Spirit was part of the Trinity godhead, and (5) the establishment of one universal church.[79]

Any other contrary teachings were declared heresy, and these involved quite a few sects with varying takes on how the Trinity worked.[80]

---

[78] The Nicene Creed touted the divinity of Jesus as part of the Trinity, whereas Arians believed Jesus was created and so did not have supreme status as God or part of the Trinity.

[79] The term "catholic" means universal, so the term Catholic Church correlates to the declared universal church.

[80] Heresy is any teaching considered false, wrong, or contrary to what was accepted by the mainstream church.

For example, Collyridianism declared that Mary and not the Holy Spirit was the third party of the Trinity and that marriage between God and Mary produced Jesus.

Those who disagreed with the Nicene Creed could die for it at the end of a sword. Just a few years later, Priscillian, Bishop of Avila, earned this fate, making him the first Christian "heretic" to be killed by other Christians.

Nicene Christianity became rooted as the state religion, while most other Christian sects faced new difficulties. Now, their persecution was being backed by the emperor *and* the church. Declared heretics and "foolish madmen" for not accepting the newly outlined beliefs, the other sects were stripped of legal status, and their property was taken by the state.

Politically speaking, Theodosius officially accepting the Nicene Trinity doctrine was a risky move. With the emperor involved in church appointments, Constantinople, a decidedly Arian city, would be tricky to keep in order. It was bad enough that different Nicene-supporting sects in Alexandria and Antioch were locked in heated opposition over the bishopric of Constantinople, keeping the city fraught with bubbling tensions. The emperor was in a religious-political minefield when it came to making appointments: inevitably, someone would be unhappy.

Even outside the empire, politics tinged religion when it came to "barbarian" tribes. Many wished to be Roman, coveting the perks of citizenship in the empire. But increasingly, they would be required to give up their old religious system and convert to Christianity if they wanted to become part of the empire.

Christianity continued its spread around the empire and beyond its borders, expanding in North Africa, the Middle East, and farther east. It became a spidery network of splintered factions and sects, many with slightly varying beliefs. Many disagreed with the main church of Rome, appointing their own leaders and formulating their own brand of Christianity.

However, while the main churches debated doctrinal issues, some tired of the arguing, politicking, and divisiveness. These left for a life of solitude, hoping to find their way back to true spirituality.

Chapter 13: Monasticism and Asceticism

Being appointed to a church position by the emperor was a big deal, and heads began to swell with pride and arrogance. Many who saw this pattern of privilege and corruption were disgusted, longing to return to a simpler, purer form of spirituality. By getting rid of material things, living an extremely frugal life, and rejecting all physical or worldly pleasures, those who chose a life of asceticism wanted fewer distractions to concentrate on spiritual matters and cultivate virtue. They worked to keep fleshly desires in check and cultivate a good name in the heavens. That meant no marriage, kids, possessions, eating food for pleasure, baths or hygienic practices, and no creature comforts. It was an exercise in extreme self-discipline designed to tame the human will and hone deep spiritual power.

Why did so many adopt such an austere, no-frills lifestyle? Reasons varied. As many spiritually-minded people saw the church taking a path towards material possessions, power, privilege, and moral corruptness, they ran in the opposite direction, looking to purify their souls and their spirituality. They wanted to leave behind the secular world and the main church in a bid for their salvation.

Some moved into isolated locations to get away from persecution and the traitors who would hand them over. But once the empire declared Christianity legal, there was no more martyrdom. Most rejoiced in that, but not all. Some had seen martyrdom as the ultimate sacrifice they could make, so now they were at a loss as to how to make the greatest sacrifice possible. So, instead of death, they essentially martyred their desires by living a life of austerity and solitude. Taking a page from the ascetics of the East, many Christians began their own monastic movement in the West.[81]

The idea of monasticism was nothing new by this point. Scriptural examples like John the Baptist, who lived in the desert eating locusts and honey, mixed with Judaism and Greco-Roman philosophy, had long formed the basis for the culture. But by the time the third and fourth centuries rolled around, monastic life looked far different and took a more prominent role as professed Christians put a new spin on it.

With such a simple lifestyle, what did ascetics do with their time? More moderate ascetics centered their lives around prayer, meditation, worship, and the basics of survival. Some begged for their basic needs while others performed manual labor, were teachers and counselors in their communities, or received visitors to impart encouragement and spiritual wisdom. Some were more extreme in their self-denial, chaining themselves to rocks and eating grass like beasts of the field. Others, like Simeon Stylites, spent decades seated on a pillar out in the open, praying. All were linked to sin, redemption, and a higher relationship with God.

Paul of Thebes, also known as Paul the Hermit, set the stage during this era. After his parents died at age sixteen, he got word that his brother-in-law was planning to betray him and turn him over to persecutors. Fleeing, he ran for safety into the desert of Thebes, Egypt. There, he survived by eating dates and drinking from a small desert oasis near his mountain home. He spent the next ninety-one years in constant prayer all day long. He set a precedent for the man that would follow him, one of the most noted models of ascetic life: Anthony the Great.[82]

Known by some as the Father of All Monks, Anthony was not the first to live a bare-bones lifestyle, but he did ignite the movement in the West. After his wealthy parents died when he was twenty years old, Anthony took the scripture in Matthew 19:21 about "selling all you have

---

[81] Those involved in monastic life were known as monks and nuns, having taken religious vows that often involved giving up worldly pleasure and material things (asceticism) and living in communal buildings like monasteries and convents.

[82] Also known as Anthony of Egypt, Anthony of the Desert, and Anthony the Hermit, among other nicknames.

and giving to the poor" very literally and entered a life of voluntary poverty under the discipleship of another hermit. A minimalist in the diet department, Anthony lived on just bread, water, and salt, with a few fasts sprinkled in throughout the week.

According to his biographer, Athanasius, Anthony had some pretty legendary experiences fighting phantasmic women and wild beast-shaped demons (who, at one point, nearly beat him to death) while living around tombs on the outskirts of his village. When he finally decided he was tired of dealing with people, he moved to a desert mountain (Mount Colzim) near the Nile River to enjoy complete solitude.

The Torment of Saint Anthony by Michaelangelo.
https://commons.wikimedia.org/wiki/File:Michelangelo_Buonarroti_-_The_Torment_of_Saint_Anthony_-_Google_Art_Project.jpg

Anthony took up residence in an abandoned Roman fort and would not set foot outside his dwelling space for the next twenty years. How did he manage to get food? The community wasn't about to let him starve, so they threw food over the wall to him. Sometimes, the faithful would make pilgrimages to see him, but he was all about solitude and refused to take any visitors. He gradually drew a following of fellow ascetically-inclined disciples who began living in huts and caves around his mountain. In time, an entire colony formed around him, and the people clamored for him to come lead them in his ways.

He finally gave in to the incessant begging and agreed to be their spiritual leader. After twenty years alone, to the surprise of his disciples, he finally emerged from the fort healthy and fit in all ways.

Until this point, monastic life was a hermit's life (called eremitic monasticism), but that was about to change. By this time, quite a large colony of monks had formed around him in the desert. He took five to six years to organize them into communities and teach them about living a life of self-denial and spirituality. After that, he returned to his desert fort and lived out the rest of his life.[83] Though he was certainly not the first to live an ascetic lifestyle, he seems to have given it momentum in Egypt, and the communities he started spread around the country and abroad. This was the beginning of communal monasticism (called cenobitic monasticism).

The monastic communities that sprang from Anthony may have been disenchanted with the church and people in general, but this was no part-time devotion or passing phase for them—they were in it all the way. Some monks and nuns even took their asceticism to great extremes, living in caves, cemeteries, swamps, solitary cells, and, in one case, a forty-foot-high pillar. One example is Amma Syncletica, a "Desert Mother" from Alexandria. Similar to Anthony, she gave away all her worldly wealth after the death of her parents and took up a hermit's residence in a crypt. She also gained quite the following and was very influential, especially among women joining the monastic movement.

---

[83] Though this time his lifestyle was less solitary. He welcomed visitors and went in and out of nearby cities. In 311 AD, he took a trip to Alexandria to encourage those being persecuted.

Amma Syncletica of Alexandria.
https://www.worldhistory.org/image/5506/amma-syncletica-of-alexandria/

Early on, most of the ascetics were lone figures, but small informal groups soon formed. One was more vulnerable to attacks by the devil when alone, so there was safety in numbers. But as the movement grew in numbers, the need for organization became more important. Enter the monk Pachomius. He saw that the men and women of these small communities needed structure and a standardized way of life. Being a former Roman soldier likely equipped him for the task.

Pachomius set up the first full-fledged monastery, where men and women lived in separate dormitory-like houses. He set up rules and regulations regarding periods of fasting, silence, reading, worship together, and prayer. Instead of following their own random perspectives on food, rest, and other daily activities, monks and nuns had jobs to support themselves in the monastery—weaving baskets, making clothes, and similar jobs.

Life was still far different from the outside, though. No one owned their own property; everything was communal. They put a hooded twist on their simple peasant-like clothes, and meals were not raucous social affairs—they were eaten together but in complete silence. Unlike regular worshippers, those in the monastic communities spent their time in meditation on the scriptures. But what about the many illiterate peasants who wanted a life of devotion in the monasteries? There was good news for them: if they entered the community, there were programs to teach them to read.

Today, many people recognize the words abbot, father, and mother in connection with those in charge of a monastery. This was also the work of Pachomius, the first to designate himself as *abba*. He established a family-like hierarchy, and everyone inside looked after one another's well-being. As appealing as that might have been to newcomers, they weren't automatically in for life. They had a long one-to-three-year probationary period to make sure they were a good fit before being allowed in permanently.

As much work as he did organizing monastic communities, Pachomius wasn't the only "father" of communal monasticism. Basil the Great, mentioned earlier, had a large hand in developing more moderate monastic guidelines to give life in the communities more balance and less austerity.

Before long, there were tens of thousands living in monastic communities. Although these seemed to be little islands unto themselves, thanks to Basil, they were connected to the larger church system. Later, monasteries would fall under the umbrella of a local church bishop. This allowed for more work to be done for the poor and needy, a cause close to Basil's heart and one he devoted much time to.

Some monks like John Chrysostom "the Golden Mouthed" and John Cassian took positions in the mainstream church. Cassian started his monastic career with three years in a hermitage before visiting other monasteries around Egypt. From there, he paved the way for monasticism in Europe.

Several years later, Cassian became involved in a big controversy with Theophilus, Archbishop of Alexandria. Again, the debate over the conception of God raged. This time, it specifically involved Origen's take on the matter. Church bishops and other leaders deemed Origen's ideas heretical as Cassian was preaching them in the West. Angered by their stance on Origen's teachings, Cassian marched to Constantinople to complain to Chrysostom and took a position in the clergy there. After exile and an appeal to Rome, Cassian gladly accepted an invitation to start a monastery in Western Europe.

When he started the first Egypt-inspired monastery in Gaul, he laid out basic rules for life. He tried to help monks in their quest for perfection by outlining their biggest obstacles and the best ways to avoid them.[84] He also took a balanced approach to monasticism. A great example is his approach to hospitality, encouraging even the most anti-social hermits to graciously entertain guests. Cassian's guidelines became the model for other Western monasteries.

The monasteries in Europe made some of the greatest contributions to spreading Christianity across the continent. While most churches were set up in cities and attracted mainly nobility and high society types, many people lived in rural locations and didn't have access to church learning. So, as monasteries popped up in farmlands and other outlying areas, Christianity gradually spread to the common people around the country. By the fourth century, monasteries became well-established and linked to the rest of Christendom.

Once pitted against the Church, monasteries increasingly became part of it. Emperors trying to control the Church founded and built monasteries, some of which became pseudo-mini states of their own. Once places to live a simple life, monasteries began a track that would lead them to become some of the wealthiest and most powerful institutions in the world.

While much of the monastic and Christian expansion had occurred in the eastern part of the Roman world until this time, Christianity was also slowly creeping towards the most western reaches of the empire.

---

[84] His work heavily influenced the monk Benedict of Nursia, founder of the widely-known Benedictine order of monks.

Chapter 14: Western Missionary Expansion and the Papacy

A sweeping trend had developed among the wealthy of large cities in Italy, Greece, Asia Minor, and North Africa. Christianity had, for many, morphed from a spiritual life journey to a faddish movement of the elite. It had become fashionable among the upper class and those looking to move up in society to join the ranks of those professing to be Christians. There was good reason. With the imperial hands in the Church pot, the wealth and prestige of the Church skyrocketed. The allure of a multitude of privileges sent many running for a position among the clergy. Aristocratic women experimented with faddish forms of devotion, much as those trying to set trends in fashion. Yet this was just a small fraction of the population. What about the common people outside high society and the epicenters of the "cultured" world?

Large swaths of rural landscape, filled with people of various cultures, languages, and identities, existed outside the wealth and nobility-filled cities of the Roman and Greek worlds. Although many lands stretching to Great Britain were technically under Roman control, they had avoided Romanization. There were no large cities in these areas at the time—not even what could be considered middle-sized cities. Barely touched by Roman influence, they were also relatively untouched by Christianity.

But as the empire had fractured into Eastern and Western parts, the Church likewise divided. Having benefited from the unification and extensive road-building projects, Christianity now traveled down the spiderweb of paths leading away from Italy and towards Gaul and beyond.[85] Word spread that Christianity welcomed people of any nation or tribe regardless of religious background. That appealed to many who liked being attached to Roman culture but didn't want to fully give up their traditional beliefs. As far as some were concerned, they could worship their gods *and* Jesus—he would make a nice addition to their pantheon of deities.

Some missionaries were making their way west in those days, but the majority of people learned about Christianity through their local grapevine—friends, relatives, and neighbors spreading the word to each other. Though Christianity was not intended to be compatible with pagan worship, the people around the empire adopted it as such.

But who was there to tell them otherwise? Most in the vast expanse of the Roman Empire were far from the educational reaches of the main Church. Thus, Christianity became as diverse as the people scattered around the far corners of the empire. By 410 AD, Christianity had reached the furthest corner—Britain.[86] But not before a few other stops.

Cannibals, beasts, barbarians—these were the ingrained ideas civilized Roman citizens had about the Germanic tribes. Given their history of savage invasion into Roman lands, these perceptions were not wholly unfounded. Bishop Optatus of North Africa expressed the views of many when he said that the "priesthood, chastity, and virginity...would not be safe" among the people of the Germanic tribes. In turn, none wanted or took the task of going out on missions to the barbarian tribes.

But the prestige of the new "Roman" religion was too much for even barbarian tribes to resist. The spread was slower in the outlying areas and was mainly organic. Migrants learned about Christianity in one place and brought it with them when the settled in another. Others learned it from Christians they kidnapped in their raids on Roman lands. Through word of mouth, the news about Christianity got around, and many Germanic people voluntarily converted.

---

[85] Late antiquity Gaul encompassed what is now France, Switzerland, Belgium, Luxembourg, and parts of the Netherlands and Germany.

[86] Some evidence shows there might have been a few Christians living in Britain as early as 250 AD.

Most preferred the controversial Arian take over the Trinitarian, especially the Goths, who had many times violently butted heads with the Roman Empire over the years. The Goths led the charge to Christianity among the Germanic tribes, and as they adopted it, a dramatic transformation began. Their previous penchant for brutal violence was gradually replaced with what contemporary historian Orosius said was a milder attitude and a tamping down on "savagery."

The conversion to Christianity wasn't without consequence for some in the Germanic world. In a wave of persecution that rivaled that under Emperor Diocletian, converted Goths were persecuted by pagan Gothic kings. The most well-known incident was perpetuated by King Wingurich, who had his men pull a chariot containing a large statue into a town with many Christian Goths. Anyone who worshipped it would be spared. But over 300, including presbyters Wereka and Batwin, refused. The king's men then trapped the Christians inside the tent of worship and set fire to the statue inside, killing everyone, including children and newborns.

Some died under persecution, and others fled to distant parts of the Roman Empire. This wasn't enough to stop the spread among the people, though. In the mid-fourth century, a prominent Christian Goth named Wulfila (who became the first Gothic bishop) worked to translate the Bible from Greek into the eastern Germanic language spoken by the Goths. As Christianity gained a strong foothold among the Goths, they passed their beliefs on to their Germanic cousins of other tribes, such as the Vandals, Franks, and Visigoths.

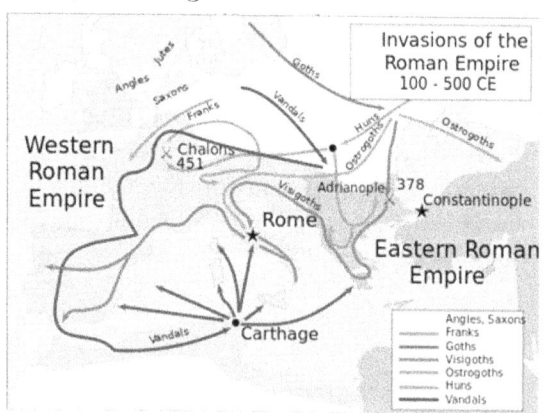

Invasions and migrations from the 2ⁿᵈ to 5ᵗʰ century.
MapMaster, CC BY-SA 2.5 <https://creativecommons.org/licenses/by-sa/2.5>, via Wikimedia Commons; https://commons.wikimedia.org/wiki/File:Invasions_of_the_Roman_Empire.svg

The details of when and how Christianity reached Gaul are a bit murky, but a mid-second-century wave of persecution in Lugdunum shows Christianity had already been established by this time.[87] That's not to say it was flourishing by any means. Surrounded by duel pagan cultures of the Gauls and Greco-Romans, Christianity was discouraged if not downright dangerous to profess, making the Christian population there rather modest.

So was the case with the first church leader of Lugdunum named Pothinus. After a mid-century plague killed thousands in Gaul, the terrified citizens were looking for a reason and someone to blame. Taking a page out of Nero's Christians-as-scapegoats book, the population decided the gods sent the plague because they were angry that the Christians refused to worship them. Pothinus was zeroed in on and promptly arrested. Before he could be tried and legally executed, some took matters into their own hands and swiftly beat him to death. He was the first martyr of Gaul but not the only. After that, church history says that forty-eight other Christians were arrested for refusing to sacrifice to Roman gods and were sent to face wild beasts in the arena.

After the death of Pothinus, Irenaeus took over the reins in Gaul, but the spread of Christianity remained slow. It was tough to make inroads in the local pagan cultures. Many in the upper classes steadfastly clung to old religions and traditions, schools celebrated pagan teachers, and the common people still looked to spells, charms, nature spirits, and divination to cure everyday ills. Many pagan festivals and customs were in place well before the Romans arrived, making them a deeply entrenched part of who the Gauls were.

In the mid-fourth century, Martin of Tours made it his aim to root the pagan idolatry out of the countryside. This became easier among the poorer population as monasteries cropped up. Martin established a "grand monastery," and Cassian later built two more. The close proximity of ascetics living a simple life similar to that of the poor yet freely practicing Christianity fostered the slow spread of Christianity in the area and beyond.

As early as the first century, the apostle Paul at least intended to go to Spain (Romans 15:24), but there is no confirmation that he ever reached

---

[87] Many Gallic saints of the period were of Greek origin, so likely Christianity had reached the area through Greek missionaries or migrants.

the Iberian Peninsula. But sometime between his life and 180 AD, at least a small community of Christians had developed, as Irenaeus made reference to. These had probably reached Spain in the process of fleeing wars in Jerusalem. A hundred years later, Cyprian of Carthage mentioned Christians in at least four cities on the peninsula. As with the rest of Western Europe, Christianity gradually spread through neighbors, families, and friends.

The earlier sporadic Christian persecutions didn't reach the small communities in Iberia, but when Diocletian's fierce sweep came, Iberian Christians suffered with the rest. The first recorded martyr was young Eulalia, said to be about years old. Despite her mother's best efforts to keep her sequestered, Eulalia snuck out and publicly proclaimed herself a Christian. Not content with just that, she also directly insulted the gods and the emperor, declaring:

"Isis, Apollo, and Venus are nothing, Maximian himself is nothing; They are nothing, because they were made by hands, He, because he reveres the works of hands."

Her stand resulted in her being stripped naked, tortured, and tied to the stake to be burned. Defiant to the very end, as the flames kicked up and smoke entered her lungs, she continued to taunt her executioners until her last dying breath.

Iberian Christians weren't the only ones mentioned by Irenaeus. He also spoke about a community among the Celts in Britain. Interestingly, it was probably the Romans themselves who brought Christianity to the furthest reaches of their empire. As early as the first century, Britain was trading with Romee. So, when Roman merchants made their way to the isles for commerce, they also brought stories about Jesus and his disciples.

However, Christianity had hardly gotten a foothold in Britain before it was nearly wiped off the isles. When the Anglo-Saxons invaded Britain in the early 400s AD, they brought their Germanic polytheism and all but replaced Christianity. The few Christians remaining fled into Wales, Ireland, and Scotland, where they continued to thrive virtually undisturbed. But in England, it would take another 200 years before Christianity would again be reestablished.

Back in the thick of the Roman Empire, things were heating up between Rome, Constantinople, Alexandria, Antioch, and Jerusalem, each of which believed they held the right as the primary church. The position of pope didn't officially exist yet, but each bishop threw in his claim as the rightful head of the Church.[88]

As the city where the first Christian congregation was established and the central governing body (council) was housed, Jerusalem was highly important to professed Christians of the early centuries. It was also the city where Jesus died and was resurrected. Many held the city as a beacon of Christian honor and prestige.

Alexandria was a veritable Christian think tank, a key city that believed itself to be the root of Christian theology. From that city, Christianity spread to Europe, but most notably to Africa and Asia. Along with Antioch, Alexandria claimed solid connections to the apostle Peter. Antioch claimed that Peter was the bishop of their city before he even joined the congregation in Rome. In addition to Peter, Alexandria also laid claim to Mark, who was said to have founded the congregation there.

Constantinople, as the newly minted capital of the Eastern Roman Empire (or "New Rome," as it was labeled), was backed by imperial power. In 381, the First Council of Constantinople declared Constantinople just under Rome in the hierarchy of important cities. Rome, nervous about the rising power of Constantinople, took exception to it being so highly honored. At a synod the next year, Damascus I protested the rise of Constantinople. As a relatively young city—only fifty years old—why should it take precedence over the much older cities of Alexandria and Antioch, where Christianity had been established much longer?

By 354, Rome's prominence continued to rise when it was billed "the Apostolic See," a reference to Peter's connection. Damascus used the words of Matthew 16:18, "You are Peter and on this rock I will build my congregation (church)," as a precedent to support the supremacy of the bishop of Rome's position.

Even as Rome's imperial power was declining, its religious power was steadily rising. It was becoming harder to argue with Rome's religious power when it was backed by three emperors. Theodosius II, Valentinian III, and Justinian all positioned the bishop of Rome as "the

---

[88] Although the term "pope" was used as early as the second and third centuries by some churches, the title "pope" for the head of the Roman Catholic Church wasn't official until about the ninth century.

Rector of the whole Church." There was still no official papal position, but the power of Rome's bishop was being cemented—even more so when Innocent I, a bishop of Rome, claimed that all major decisions should be referred to Rome's authority. This gave Damascus I the backing to have himself styled the "Supreme Pontiff" in 380 AD.[89]

Yet with the other cities posing powerful threats to its supremacy, Rome needed to ensure its head position was secured and that the other sees[90] clearly understood it. This was made easier by Rome's close relationship with the emperors, who steadily conferred more and more power to the bishops there. In 440 AD, Roman bishop Leo I used Roman law to his advantage and solidified the position: the bishops of Rome were legally declared the successors of Peter.

When the matter came up again during the Council of Chalcedon in 451 AD, Leo I claimed he was "speaking with the voice of Peter." To quell the discontent of Constantinople, the council again reaffirmed that it stood only second to Rome. However, Rome took exception to this renewed declaration since it did not recognize Rome's authority over Constantinople (or any other see, for that matter). Yet Rome held firm to its position.

The battle for supremacy continued for centuries, coming to a head in the eleventh century. Disagreement over the prime position created the Great Schism of 1054, putting Rome and Constantinople on opposing sides of the divide, each believing they should hold the right to the top position in the Church. Even though Rome's position was well affirmed, debates over the supremacy of the papacy continued throughout the Middle Ages and even into the mid-twentieth century.

---

[89] Or *Pontifus Maximus,* a term used for leaders, particularly emperors, within the Roman Empire's pagan religious order.

[90] From the Latin word *sedes,* meaning "seat," the word see refers to the position of bishop of a city.

Bonus Chapter: Art

Fascinating, storied, and at times bewildering in its meaning, early Christian art melded symbols, classic Greco-Roman imagery, and biblical history into paintings, mosaics, sculptures, and even sarcophagi (coffin-like boxes made of stone).

Many have seen the grand stained-glass depictions and famed Christian-themed art of medieval times, but why is Christian art from the first century never talked about? Because it hardly exists. It's not that early Christians had anything against art, per se, but they had reason not to create it in their early days.

Most early Christians were of Jewish background, and no doubt the words of the Mosaic law were indelibly pressed into their minds, particularly the commandments against forming any images of God, idolatrous depictions of "anything under heaven and earth," and to "be on guard against every form of idolatry." [91]To be fair, much of the Greco-Roman art surrounding first-century Christians had to do with idolatry and pagan worship, so it stands to reason that they would avoid creating any kind of art that could break those commandments.

There was a second practical reason for their silence in the art world: Christianity was not very popular and was even banned for a time. Would people trying to lay low and not make themselves a target for increased persecution be openly painting and sculpting about the things they were outlawed for? Apparently not.

---

[91] There are no artistic images of God in the early Christian art of the Roman Empire.

But their creativity wasn't under wraps for long, as Christians found ways to work around the pesky bans and create art that didn't draw the attention of Roman authorities. Some art simply featured stories from the biblical history of the Jews. Stories such as Noah and the Ark and the prophet Samuel anointing David as king portrayed religious figures that expressed their faith but wouldn't be particularly concerning to the Romans.

Samuel anointing David as king.
https://commons.wikimedia.org/wiki/File:Dura_Synagogue_WC3_David_anointed_by_Samuel.jpg

Sometimes, Christians disguised their beliefs with artistic symbolism. Themes of death and resurrection could not be openly portrayed, but other Bible stories, such as Jonah and the Whale, were used to depict touchier topics.

Jonah being thrown into the sea.
https://commons.wikimedia.org/wiki/File:Jonah_thrown_into_the_Sea.jpg

At times, Christians adopted pagan symbols and gave them Christian meaning. Many early works of art contain elements borrowed from ancient pagan religions, like the mother and child, bulls, lions, and peacocks. Why peacocks? It was believed that their flesh never rotted, so many cultures regarded them as a symbol of eternal life.

Not all symbols of Christianity were borrowed from other religions or cultures; some were decidedly their own. The fish symbol was born from an acronym of the words "Jesus Christ God's Son Savior." The first letter of each word in Greek spells out the word Ichthus (ΙΧΘΥΣ), the Greek word for fish.

Another workaround Christians used was to depict figures under classic Roman disguises (think togas and Roman haircuts instead of fake noses and glasses). A great example is a painting called "The Good Shepherd."

Good Shepherd from the Catacomb of Priscilla, 250–300.
https://commons.wikimedia.org/wiki/File:Good_shepherd_01_small.jpg

As a Jew, Jesus would have worn Jewish garb with fringes and sported a beard, as all Jewish men of the time. But here, he is depicted as a beardless shepherd wearing a toga—two distinctly Greco-Roman features.

Another painting shows Jesus looking like the Greek Orpheus, a demi-god with a supernatural talent for music and writing.

Jesus depicted as Orpheus.
https://commons.wikimedia.org/wiki/File:Christ-Orpheus_from_Rome_catacombe.jpg

Disguise wasn't the only reason Christian art featured things that were out of place for Jews and Christians. They also hadn't developed their own distinct style and borrowed from what they knew of art at the time— classic Greco-Roman features and even characteristics and symbols plucked from ancient Egyptian and Babylonian art. An example is a highly ornate sarcophagus made shortly after the Edict of Milan legalized Christianity. In the middle, Jesus' father Joseph, a Jew, is given a very Roman look. The angels were not immune to a little fine-tuning of their image—they, too, are given togas.

When Christians couldn't openly portray their art above ground, some of the most important works of early Christian art were found underground. The extensive catacombs of Rome held a virtual treasure trove of art in a place easily hidden from public view.[92] Sarcophagi, like the one above, were just the tip of the artistic iceberg. Paintings, mosaics, carvings, and even gold glass were used to portray religious figures and scenes.

Often, though, art proclaimed the faith of the deceased, sometimes in engravings of semi-cryptic phrases like "to the well-deserving." Symbolic images might be used alongside the text to express the faith of the dead and their family.

Other times, the faith of the deceased was expressed in painting. An example is the "Veiled Woman," who is depicted with arms outstretched in prayer.

The Veiled Woman.
Original image by Kristicak. Uploaded by Kim Martins, published on 01 April 2019. The copyright holder has published this content under the following license: Creative Commons Attribution-ShareAlike; https://www.worldhistory.org/image/10353/the-cubiculum-of-the-veiled-woman/

After Christianity was legalized, there was, understandably, a great shift in Christian art and its content—less disguise and more overt painting depicting Jesus in various scenes from his life.

---

[92] Underground passages with chambers and insets used for burying the dead.

Jesus healing the woman with the flow of blood.
https://commons.wikimedia.org/wiki/File:Healing_of_a_bleeding_women_Marcellinus-Peter-Catacomb.jpg

Mosaic of Jesus preaching, Rome.
Welleschik, CC BY-SA 3.0 <https://creativecommons.org/licenses/by-sa/3.0>, via Wikimedia Commons;
https://commons.wikimedia.org/wiki/File:Apsis_mosaic,_Santa_Pudenziana,_Rome_W3.JPG

As Rome and Christianity grew closer, that relationship also became reflected in Christian art. In a nod to the emperor, Jesus is shown treading on a lion in a style very similar to imperial sculptures.

Christ treading the beasts.
José Luiz Bernardes Ribeiro;
<https://commons.wikimedia.org/wiki/File:Christ_treading_the_beasts_-_Chapel_of_Saint_Andrew_-_Ravenna_2016.jpg>

Despite so much upheaval and instability in the world of Christians, the spread of Christianity had unexpected impacts on the creative world. Creations emerged that made a deep and lasting impact on art history, not just in Europe but around the globe. The influence of early Christian art left imprints that could be seen throughout European art into the Renaissance.

Conclusion

Christianity has had a long journey from the beginning of the first century until now. Today, it is one of the major branches of religion in the world with over 2.3 billion people professing to be Christian—that is over a quarter of the world's population. From its origins, it has gone through many changes, some of which Jesus himself prophesied would happen.

Throughout two millennia, Christianity changed the shape of culture, religion, and, in many instances, history, though in many ways that was not the original intention. Early Christianity was not just a religion or a fad but an entire lifestyle, one that thousands eagerly adopted. Those who followed it adhered to tenets such as love, unselfishness, and virtue, among other things, not just during special times or rituals but also as a part of everyday life. They worked to apply the lessons Jesus taught to make real and true changes to themselves for the better. And they shared that message because they wanted others to have a better life and real hope for a better future.

Reading about the progression of Christianity from the first apostles to small groups of disciples to the organization of larger congregations that spread around the Roman Empire is more than just a story; it's the historical heritage of millions. Within that are thousands of real people with many beautiful, heartbreaking, and, at times, terrifying experiences. These stories make up the mosaic of early Christianity.

The message that they preached was based on a strong, enduring hope, not blind faith or wishful thinking. Despite the many changes to

Christianity that have come over the centuries, the original teachings of Jesus and the early Christians still exist within the Bible. That message endures to this day and gives billions of people hope for a better and brighter world.

Here's another book by Enthralling History that you might like

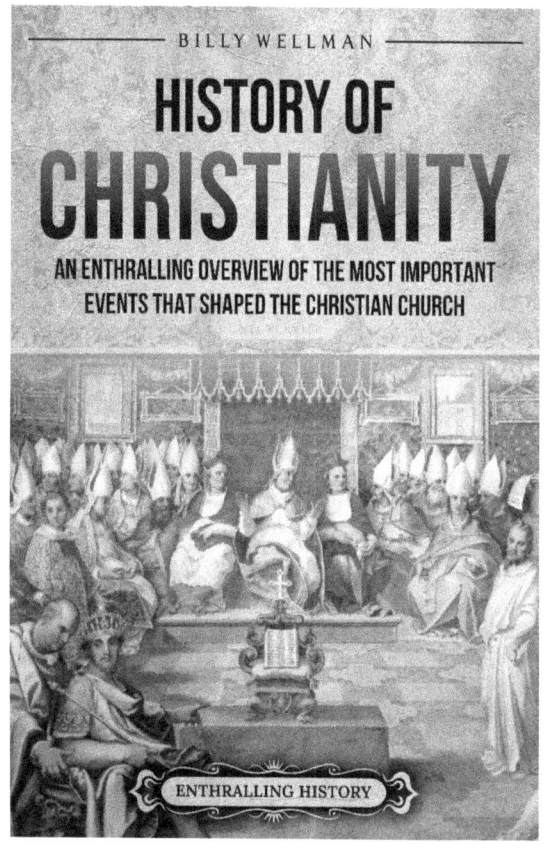

Free limited time bonus

Stop for a moment. We have a free bonus set up for you. The problem is this: we forget 90% of everything that we read after 7 days. Crazy fact, right? Here's the solution: we've created a printable, 1-page pdf summary for this book that you're reading now. All you have to do to get your free pdf summary is to go to the following website:

https://livetolearn.lpages.co/enthrallinghistory/

Once you do, it will be intuitive. Enjoy, and thank you!

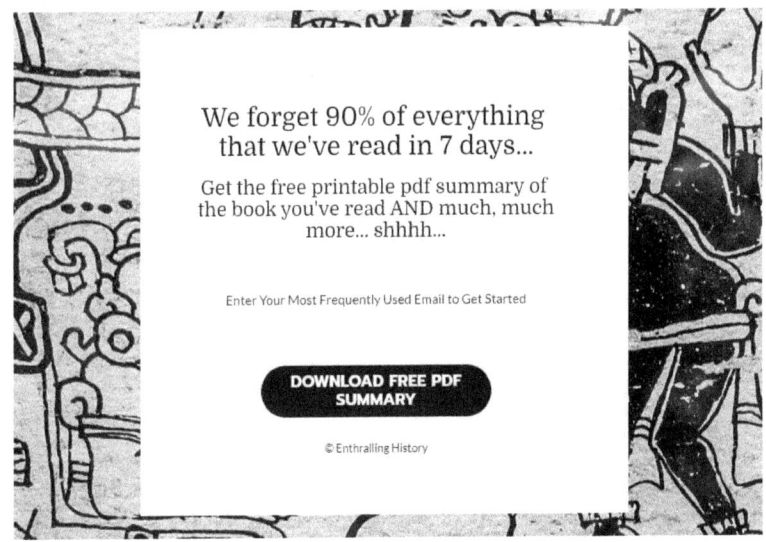

References

Edersheim, Alfred (1904) *The Life and Times of Jesus the Messiah*. London: Longmans, Green and Co.

Insight on the Scriptures, Volume 2 p. 387. Messiah. Watchtower Bible and Tract Society of Pennsylvania. https://wol.jw.org

Encyclopedia Judaica Vol.05 (2007) Fred Skolnik, Editor in Chief Michael Berenbaum, Executive Editor

Judaism in the First Century (2009) Yale Courses. The Jews, Hellenization, and the Maccabees

https://www.jewishvirtuallibrary.org/the-ancient-greeks-and-the-jews-jewish-virtual-library

https://www.historytoday.com/archive/jews-greeks-and-romans

The Hellenization of the Jews. GH Gilbert. American Journal of Theology (1909) https://www.journals.uchicago.edu/doi/pdf/10.1086/478870

A Historical Atlas of the Jewish People: From the Time of the Patriarchs to the Present. Eli Barnavi (Editor). Schocken Books.

Knight, George Angus Fulton. "Maccabees". *Encyclopedia Britannica*, https://www.britannica.com/topic/Maccabees. Accessed 20 July 2022.

Pompey's Siege of Jerusalem. Jona Lendering. https://www.livius.org/articles/concept/roman-jewish-wars/

Flavius Josephus, Jewish War Volume 2

The Jewish Encyclopedia. (1976, Vol. VIII, p. 508)

Britannica, The Editors of Encyclopedia. "Gospel According to Matthew". Encyclopedia Britannica, https://www.britannica.com/topic/Gospel-According-to-Matthew. Accessed 21 July 2022.

All Scripture Is Inspired of God and Beneficial. Watchtower Bible and Tract Society of Pennsylvania.

The Ecclesiastical History, Eusebius, of Caesarea, Bishop of Caesarea. Published 1942 Cambridge, Mass.: Harvard University Press

The Cyclopedia of Biblical, Theological, and Ecclesiastical Literature. James Strong and John McClintock; Haper and Brothers; NY https://www.biblicalcyclopedia.com/

The Slaughter of the Innocents https://biblearchaeology.org/research/new-testament-era/2411-the-slaughter-of-the-innocents-historical-fact-or-legendary-fiction

w12 4/1 pp. 18-19 ◻ Apocryphal Gospels—Hidden Truths About Jesus?

Caesar Augustus: An Archaeological Biography December 13, 2019 Bryan Windle https://biblearchaeologyreport.com/2019/12/13/caesar-augustus-an-archaeological-biography/

New Catholic Encyclopedia (1967) page 918. New York: McGraw-Hill Book Company

The Greatest Man Who Ever Lived. Watchtower Bible and Tract Society of Pennsylvania

Herod Archelaus https://en.wikipedia.org/wiki/Herod_Archelaus last edited on 21 August 2022

Bible Translations:

New World Translation

Byington Version

Kingdom Interlinear Version

King James Version

"Sea of Galilee Boat (Jesus Boat)". Madain Project. Retrieved 1 September 2022. https://web.archive.org/web/20200929210904/https://madainproject.com/boat_of_jesus

The Imperial Bible Dictionary (1866) Cross, Crucify page 376. London: Blackie and Son.

"Bearing Thorough Witness" About God's Kingdom. Watchtower Bible and Tract Society of Pennsylvania

The Germans of Galacia https://sites.ualberta.ca/~german/AlbertaHistory/Galicians.htm

Britannica, The Editors of Encyclopedia. "Phrygia". Encyclopedia Britannica, https://www.britannica.com/place/Phrygia. Accessed 9 October 2022.

Macedonian History https://macedonian.org/our-culture/macedonian-history/

Konstan, David, "Epicurus", *The Stanford Encyclopedia of Philosophy* (Fall 2022 Edition), Edward N. Zalta & Uri Nodelman (eds.) https://plato.stanford.edu/archives/fall2022/entries/epicurus/

Baltzly, Dirk, "Stoicism", *The Stanford Encyclopedia of Philosophy* (Spring 2019 Edition), Edward N. Zalta (ed.) https://plato.stanford.edu/archives/spr2019/entries/stoicism/

Christopher W. Blackwell, "The Council of the Areopagus," in C.W. Blackwell, ed., *Dēmos: Classical Athenian Democracy* (A. Mahoney and R. Scaife, ed., *The Stoa: A Consortium for Electronic Publication in the Humanities* [http://www.stoa.org]) edition of January 26, 2003.

Cartwright, M. (2009, September 02). Corinth. *World History Encyclopedia*. Retrieved from https://www.worldhistory.org/corinth/ October 3, 2022.

Lystra https://www.allaboutturkey.com/lystra.html

Cartwright, M. (2016, May 04). Philippi. *World History Encyclopedia*. Retrieved from https://www.worldhistory.org/Philippi/ October 3, 2022.

Cartwright, M. (2016, May 01). Thessalonica. *World History Encyclopedia*. Retrieved from https://www.worldhistory.org/Thessalonica/ October 3, 2022

"Greek Language, Early Christian and Byzantine." New Catholic Encyclopedia. Retrieved February 04, 2023 from Encyclopedia.com: https://www.encyclopedia.com/religion/encyclopedias-almanacs-transcripts-and-maps/greek-language-early-christian-and-byzantin

Kelly, John N.D. "Apologist". Encyclopedia https://www.britannica.com/topic/Apologist. Accessed 1 February 2023.

Lévy, Carlos, "Philo of Alexandria", *The Stanford Encyclopedia of Philosophy* (Fall 2022 Edition), Edward N. Zalta & Uri Nodelman (eds.), URL = <https://plato.stanford.edu/archives/fall2022/entries/philo/>.

Santrac, Aleksandar S. (2013). Three I know not what: The influence of Greek philosophy on the doctrine of Trinity. In die Skriflig, 47(1), 1-7. Retrieved February 11, 2023, from http://www.scielo.org.za/scielo.php?script=sci_arttext&pid=S2305-08532013000100059&lng=en&tlng=en.

Ruben Ortega | 9 June, 2016 | Chronology, Expansion of Christianity, The Life of Early Christians https://www.earlychristians.org/the-life-of-early-christians/

J. Warner Wallace Published May 18, 2020 Lessons for Today's Church from the Life of the Early Church https://coldcasechristianity.com/writings/lessons-for-todays-church-from-the-life-of-the-early-church/.

Jonas, Hans "Gnosticism. " Encyclopedia of Philosophy. Retrieved March 04, 2023 from Encyclopedia.com: https://www.encyclopedia.com/humanities/encyclopedias-almanacs-transcripts-and-maps/gnosticism

"Gnosticism" by Edward Moore, *The Internet Encyclopedia of Philosophy*, ISSN 2161-0002, https://iep.utm.edu/, March 4, 2023

Britannica, T. Editors of Encyclopedia *Ebionite*. *Encyclopedia Britannica*. https://www.britannica.com/topic/Ebionites

Arendzen, J. (1909). Ebionites. In The Catholic Encyclopedia. New York: Robert Appleton Company. Retrieved March 12, 2023 from New Advent: http://www.newadvent.org/cathen/05242c.htm

Krauss, Samuel. "Nazarenes". *Jewish Encyclopedia*. Retrieved 2023-03-23. jewishencyclopedia.com.

David Eastman (Translations & Introductions). *The Ancient Martyrdom Accounts of Peter and Paul*. (SBL Press: Atlanta, 2015).

Britannica, T. Editors of Encyclopedia). *St. Clement I. Encyclopedia Britannica*. https://www.britannica.com/biography/Saint-Clement-I

Catholic Online, Pope St. Clement I https://www.catholic.org/saints/saint.php?saint_id=37

Catholic Encyclopedia (1913) Pope St. Clement I by Henry Palmer Chapman, https://en.wikisource.org/wiki/Catholic_Encyclopedia_(1913)/Pope_St._Clement_I

John Malham, Foxs Book of Martyrs (1856)

The Martyrdom of Polycarp. Translated by J.B. Lightfoot. Abridged and modernized by Stephen Tomkins. Edited and prepared for the web by Dan Graves. https://christianhistoryinstitute.org/study/module/polycarp

Watchtower Bible and Tract Society 'Away with the Godless!' w89 11/15 pp. 21-23

Wingren, G. (April 8, 2023). St. Irenaeus. Encyclopedia Britannica. https://www.britannica.com/biography/Irenaeus

Irenaeus of Lyons, Grant, Robert M. (Robert McQueen), 1917-2014 London ; New York : Routledge

Britannica, T. Editors of Encyclopedia (Invalid Date). *Saint Hippolytus of Rome. Encyclopedia Britannica*. https://www.britannica.com/biography/Saint-Hippolytus-of-Rome

The Ante-Nicene Fathers: The Writings of the Fathers down to A.D.325 (1995) Peabody (Mass.): Hendrickson

Maritano, Mario, "Basileiad", in: Brill Encyclopedia of Early Christianity Online, General Editor David G. Hunter, Paul J.J. van Geest, Bert Jan Lietaert Peerbolte. Consulted online on 20 May 2023 http://dx.doi.org/10.1163/2589-7993_EECO_SIM_00000395

Kraft, Heinrich, Early Christian Thinkers: An Intro to Clement of Alexandria and Origen (1964) New York: Association Pr.

Pedrozo, José M. "The Brothers of Jesus and his Mother's Virginity." *The Thomist: A Speculative Quarterly Review* 63, no. 1 (1999): 83-104. https://doi.org/10.1353/tho.1999.0044.

Who Was Mary Magdalene? Bible Questions Answered p. 172 Watchtower Bible and Tract Society of Pennsylvania

Britannica, T. Editors of Encyclopedia (Invalid Date). St. Mary Magdalene. Encyclopedia Britannica. https://www.britannica.com/biography/Saint-Mary-Magdalene

F.F. Bruce, "Christianity Under Claudius," Bulletin of the John Rylands Library 44 (March 1962): 309-326.

Clugnet, Léon. "St. Catherine of Alexandria." The Catholic Encyclopedia. Vol. 3. New York: Robert Appleton Company, 1908. 6 Jun. 2023 <http://www.newadvent.org/cathen/03445a.htm>.

Britannica, T. Editors of Encyclopedia St. Barbara. Encyclopedia Britannica. https://www.britannica.com/biography/Saint-Barbara

Mark Galli (1990) Persecution in the Early Church: A Gallery of the Persecuting Emperors https://christianhistoryinstitute.org/magazine/article/persecution-in-early-church-gallery

"Nero Persecutes the Christians, 64 A.D." EyeWitness to History, www.eyewitnesstohistory.com (2000).

Mark Wilson (May 4, 2023) Alternative Facts: Domitian's Persecution of Christians, https://www.biblicalarchaeology.org/daily/biblical-topics/post-biblical-period/domitian-persecution-of-christians/

The Works of Josephus, translated by William Whiston, Hendrickson Publishers, 1987

Keresztes, P. (1968). Marcus Aurelius a Persecutor? *Harvard Theological Review, 61*(3), 321-341. doi:10.1017/S0017816000029230

The Acts of the Christian Martyrs, texts and translation by Herbert Musurillo. (c) Oxford University Press, 1972

Paul Johnson (1928) A History of Christianity. New York: Atheneum

Constantine the Great—A Champion of Christianity? (1998) Watchtower Bible and Tract Society of Pennsylvania

Carroll, Warren (1987), The Building of Christendom, Front Royal VA: Christendom College Press, retrieved July 24, 2023

Knox, J. S. (2016, August 23). The Monastic Movement: Origins & Purposes. *World History Encyclopedia*. Retrieved from https://www.worldhistory.org/article/930/the-monastic-movement-origins--purposes/

5 Ways Christianity Spread Through Ancient Rome, Becky Little. HISTORY. A&E Television Networks. Accessed September 8, 2023 https://www.history.com/news/5-ways-christianity-spread-through-ancient-rome

Fletcher, R.A. The barbarian conversion: from paganism to Christianity (1999) Berkeley, Calif.: University of California Press

Dietz, Maribel (2005). Wandering Monks, Virgins, and Pilgrims: Ascetic Travel in the Mediterranean World, A.D. 300-800. Pennsylvania State University Press.

Dr. Allen Farber, "Early Christian art," in *Smarthistory*, August 8, 2015, accessed September 26, 2023, https://smarthistory.org/early-christian-art/.

Dr. Allen Farber, "Santa Pudenziana," in *Smarthistory*, August 16, 2023, accessed September 26, 2023, https://smarthistory.org/santa-pudenziana/.

Jason David BeDuhn, Truth in Translation. University Press of America 2003.

www.ingramcontent.com/pod-product-compliance
Lightning Source LLC
Chambersburg PA
CBHW070334010526
44107CB00004B/500